MY PICTURE STORY BIBLE

Written by Marion Thomas *Illustrated by* Honor Ayres

THE OLD TESTAMENT Page 5

THE NEW TESTAMENT Page 187

INDEX Page 312

For Alana, Lydia and Sam

First edition 2012
Flying Frog Publishing
Lutherville, MD 21093

Copyright © 2012 Anno Domini Publishing
www.ad-publishing.com

Text copyright © 2012 Anno Domini Publishing, Marion Thomas
Illustrations copyright © 2012 Honor Ayres

Editorial Director Annette Reynolds
Art Director Gerald Rogers
Pre-production Krystyna Kowalska Hewitt
Production John Laister

All rights reserved

Printed and bound in China

MY
PICTURE STORY
BIBLE

Written by Marion Thomas Illustrated by Honor Ayres

THE OLD TESTAMENT

In the beginning

Genesis 1:1-8

At first there was nothing, nothing at all. Everything was dark. Then God said, "Let there be light!" And suddenly there was light in all the dark spaces and God saw that it was good. He called the light "day" and the darkness "night." Then God separated the sky above and the waters below.

God makes plants and trees
Genesis 1:9-13

God gathered the waters together so
that there was land and sea, beaches and
splashing waves. God liked what He saw. But
then He filled it with plants and trees and fruit
and flowers, and He liked it even more.

God makes the sun, moon, and stars

Genesis 1:14-19

God made the hot sun to shine in the day and the silvery moon to shine at night. He scattered stars in the night sky to sparkle in the darkness. And God saw that this was good.

God makes fish and sea creatures

Genesis 1:20-23

God filled the salty seas with creatures large and small. Some had fins and tails to swim, while others bumped or crawled along the sea bed. Some floated around and others leapt out of the waters into the air above.

God makes birds and butterflies

Genesis 1:20-23

God filled the skies with every kind of winged and feathered creature. Many bore beautiful colors and filled the air with sound. Others were soft and delicate and silent. God saw that all that He had made was good.

God makes all the animals

Genesis 1:24-25

God filled His world with every kind of animal to live on the land. There were elephants and giraffes, tigers and chameleons, crocodiles and hippos. Now God's world was full of chattering sounds, colorful creatures, and the smell of scented flowers and trees. God was very pleased with all that He had made.

God makes people

Genesis 1:26-31

Then God made a man and a woman—people to take care of everything else He had made. The people were different. God could talk to them and they could talk to Him. They could think and feel, share and be happy. They could love as God loved all that He had made. God saw that it was very, very good.

God rests

Genesis 2:1-3

God had made the heavens and the earth and filled it with all the living creatures, big and small, soft and furry, hard and spiky. He had made the trees and plants so they would produce fruit and cover the land. Everything was good. Everything was beautiful. So God stopped there—and rested from the work of creation.

The garden of Eden

Genesis 2:8-17

The first people God made were his friends. Adam and Eve lived in a garden in Eden. God gave them everything they needed. A river with clear, cool water ran through the garden. The trees were full of good food to eat. "But don't eat from the tree in the middle of the garden," God warned them.

The sneaky serpent
Genesis 3:1-13

"Did God tell you not to eat from that tree?" whispered a serpent one day. Eve looked at the ripe, juicy fruit. She picked some and tasted it. It was good. Then she gave some to Adam. But as soon as they had eaten the fruit, Adam and Eve realized they had broken the rule God gave them. They were so ashamed, they hid.

Everything is spoiled

Genesis 3:14-24

God knew what Adam and Eve had done. He had trusted the people he had made, but they had chosen to disobey him. Now Adam and Eve were unhappy. God was unhappy, too. God told them they would have to leave the beautiful garden. Nothing would be the same again.

Adam and Eve's children

Genesis 4:1-5

Adam and Eve had two sons. Cain grew plants for food. Abel kept sheep and goats. "God has been kind to us," said Abel, looking at all his lambs. "Let's take him gifts." Abel offered God his best lamb. Cain offered some of his grain. God saw that Abel had a good heart. God saw that Cain did not.

Cain and Abel

Genesis 4:6-9

Cain was jealous of his brother. He sulked. "Be careful," said God. "Don't let your bad temper take control of you." But Cain did not listen to God. He asked Abel to walk in the field with him and then Cain killed him. "Where is your brother?" God asked Cain. "I don't know," lied Cain. "Am I his keeper?"

Cain kills his brother

Genesis 4:10-15

"What have you done?" said God. "Your brother cries out to me from the earth where you have killed him. You must leave this place. You will always feel guilty for what you have done. You will never know peace." Cain was frightened. "Please don't punish me like this," he asked God. "I will let no one hurt you," said God. "I will keep you safe."

God's plan

Genesis 6:5-17

God had made a perfect world. But the people He had made were not always kind to each other. Before long they were all cheating and hurting, fighting and stealing. There was only one good man left. His name was Noah. God told Noah that soon a flood would come and destroy everything on the earth.

Noah builds an ark

Genesis 6:18-22

Noah had a wife and three grown-up sons. His sons had wives. Noah was a very old man when God spoke to him about the ark. But Noah trusted God. He started to cut down the trees to make the logs to make the boat. He did everything that God had told him to, until the ark was built. It took a very long time.

Two by two

Genesis 7:1-9

God told Noah to find pairs of creatures, great and small, to be kept safe from the floodwaters, so there would be plenty to start to build God's world again. The animals came to Noah and boarded the ark through the door, two by two. Then Noah's family followed them inside.

The flood

Genesis 7:10-12, 17-24

God shut the door of the ark. And then the rain came down. Slowly, steadily, little drops and big drops of cool rain fell, hour after hour, day after day. The rain drummed on the roof, it bounced on the rivers, and it soaked into the earth. Soon the waters covered the land. Then they covered the treetops. But the ark floated above it all.

The raven and the dove

Genesis 8:6-11

After forty days and forty nights, there was silence. No rain drummed on the roof. Noah waited patiently while the wind blew outside. Then he set free a raven—but the bird did not return. Noah waited a bit more and then set free a dove. When she returned, Noah saw that she was carrying a fresh, green olive leaf!

Leaving the ark

Genesis 8:15-19

Now Noah knew that the trees were growing again. The ark settled on Mount Ararat while the flood waters went down bit by bit. When the land was dry again, God told Noah to open up the door. All the birds and animals trotted out of the ark and went to find new homes in the new world God had given them. They were free.

The rainbow

Genesis 8:20-22; 9:12-17

Then Noah made an altar and he thanked God for keeping him safe, with his family and all the animals. A beautiful rainbow appeared in the sky. "I will never destroy the earth by flood again," God said. "Whenever you see a rainbow, remember—this is my promise."

God speaks to Abraham

Genesis 12:1-4

Years had passed and people had once more filled the land. God spoke to Abraham. "I have chosen you, Abraham. I will make your family into a great nation and I will bless you. Move from your home here and I will show you where to go."

A home in Canaan

Genesis 12:5

Abraham was already an old man. He had a wife and nephew, servants, sheep, goats, and camels. He didn't know where they were going, and he didn't know how long it would take to get there, but Abraham trusted God. He packed up his tents and began the journey across the hot, dusty desert.

God blesses Abraham

Genesis 12:7

When Abraham reached Canaan, he saw that it was a land made green by water. It was a good place to make his home. "I will bless you," God said to him. "This land will belong to your children and all your family. You will have as many descendants as there are stars in the sky."

Three special visitors

Genesis 18:1-10

Abraham knew that God kept his promises. But he wondered how he could have many descendants when he and his wife, Sarah, still had no child of their own. Then one hot day, three men came to visit Abraham. He soon realized that they came with a message from God himself. Abraham made his visitors welcome.

Little baby Isaac

Genesis 21:1-6

The visitors told Abraham that Sarah would hold her baby son in her arms when they visited in one year's time. Sarah laughed when she heard the news. She thought it must surely be too late now. But God kept his promise. Abraham and Sarah soon had a little boy named Isaac, which means "laughter."

A sad day for Abraham

Genesis 22:1-6

Isaac grew into a strong boy. He made his parents very happy. Then one day Abraham heard God speak to him again. What was God asking? Surely God couldn't mean it? Yet Abraham loved God. He trusted Him… Abraham and Isaac went up the mountain to offer God a very special gift.

The very special gift
Genesis 22:7-12

"Where is the ram for the sacrifice, father?" Isaac asked him. Abraham knew that Isaac trusted him just as he trusted God. So when Abraham picked up the knife to offer his precious son back to God… Isaac was not afraid. Then, "Stop!" said an angel. Now God knew that Abraham loved and trusted Him.

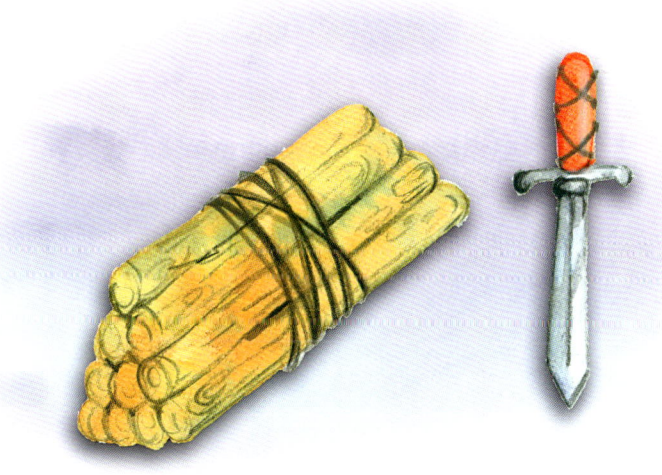

God's blessing

Genesis 22:13-18

Abraham hugged his son tightly. Then he saw a ram caught in a bush nearby. He offered God the ram as a sacrifice instead. "I know you love me, Abraham, and now I know you trust me because you obeyed me even when it was really hard. I will bless you, now and always."

A special wife for Isaac

Genesis 24:1-14

When Isaac was grown up, Abraham sent his servant to find a special girl who could be Isaac's wife, someone who was good and kind and loved God. "I will know I have the right girl," the servant prayed, "if she offers me water—and then fetches water for my ten camels too!"

The answer to a prayer

Genesis 24:15-27

When Rebekah came to the well for water, the servant thought she was very beautiful. But was she kind and good? "Let me bring you some water," she said to Abraham's servant, "and also some for your thirsty camels. It looks as if you have come from a long journey." The servant smiled. God had answered his prayer.

Two little boys

Genesis 25:24-26

Isaac married Rebekah and, after a while, God blessed them with not one, but two little boys—twins! Esau was born first. He was strong and covered with hair. Jacob came after him, holding on to Esau's heel. They were hard work for Isaac and Rebekah.

Esau and Jacob

Genesis 25:27-29

Esau grew up and learned to hunt. Isaac loved his son and was proud of him. Jacob liked to cook and spent more time with his mother. Esau would sometimes come home after a day's hunting to the smell of good food cooking in a pot.

Esau's silly promise
Genesis 25:29-34

One day Jacob cooked a tasty lentil stew. Esau could smell it long before he reached the tent. "I'd do anything for some of that stew. I'm starving!" he said. "Okay," Jacob replied. "You can have some—if you will let me take your place and have our father's blessing when the time comes." So Esau sold his birthright for a bowl of stew.

A father's blessing

Genesis 27:1-4

Isaac grew to be old and blind. He knew that soon it would be his time to die. "Esau," he said to his eldest son, "take your bow and arrow and bring back something good for me to eat. Then I will bless you before I die." So Esau left his father and went out hunting.

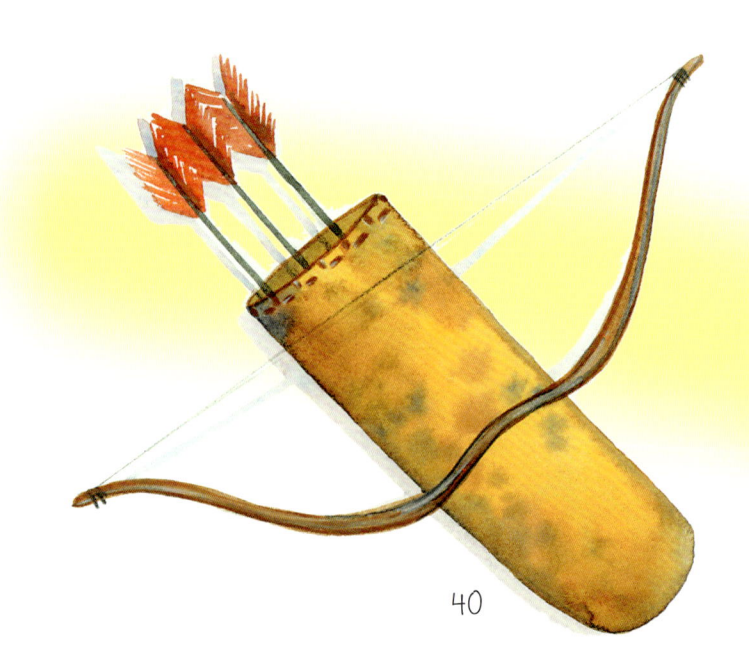

A mother's wish

Genesis 27:5-16

Rebekah knew that Esau had gone hunting. She started to cook some food for Isaac and called Jacob. "Quickly! Dress yourself in Esau's clothes," she said to her youngest son. Then, so that Jacob could pretend to be his smelly, hairy brother, she covered his arms and neck in goatskins.

Jacob tricks his father

Genesis 27:18-29

Isaac was surprised when Jacob brought the steaming food to him. "You had good luck hunting today, I think?" he asked his son. Jacob smelled like Esau. Jacob felt like Esau. So surely this must be Esau. "May God bless you and keep you. May you grow to be rich and rule over your brother," Isaac said.

Jacob is sent away

Genesis 27:30-46

When Esau returned, he asked Isaac to bless him. But it was too late. Isaac was very sorry. Esau was very angry. Rebekah was very worried! She and Isaac decided it would be best if Jacob went to stay with her brother, Laban. So Jacob left his family and traveled to the place where Laban lived with his two daughters.

Jacob's ladder

Genesis 28:10-22

Jacob slept under the stars that night with a rock for his pillow. And Jacob dreamed. In his dream he saw angels climbing up and down a ladder that led to heaven. God spoke to Jacob from heaven, promising that He would bless Jacob and take care of him as He had his father and grandfather.

Jacob falls in love

Genesis 29:1-19

When Jacob came near to his uncle's house, he saw a beautiful girl taking care of her sheep. Jacob wanted to find out everything about her. He soon discovered that she was Rachel, the daughter of his uncle, Laban. Jacob promised his uncle that he would work for him for seven years if he could marry Rachel.

Laban's unkind trick

Genesis 29:20-25

Day after day, Jacob worked for Laban. It seemed only a short time because he knew that he could marry the beautiful Rachel at the end. But after the wedding, when Jacob lifted his wife's veil, he found that Laban had married him to Leah, Rachel's older sister! Jacob was very angry. Poor Leah was very sad.

Everyone is happy!
Genesis 29:26-28

Laban told Jacob that it was the custom that the older sister must marry first. But he offered to let Jacob marry Rachel too—as long as Jacob worked another seven years looking after Laban's sheep and goats. Many people had more than one wife at that time, so Jacob was happy. He married Rachel and had two wives.

Lots of wives and children!

Genesis 29:31—30:24

God saw that Jacob loved Rachel the best, so he blessed Leah with many children. It was a long time before Rachel had two sons, too. Jacob had a large family with a daughter called Dinah and twelve little boys: Reuben, Simeon, Levi, Judah, Dan, Naphtali, Gad, Asher, Issachar, Zebulun, Joseph, and Benjamin.

Time to go home

Genesis 30:25-36

Jacob had been with Laban a long time. He wanted to go home. But Laban knew that while Jacob was there, God was blessing him. "Don't go yet," said naughty Uncle Laban. "Wait until you have a big herd of speckled or spotted sheep and goats." Then Laban hid the spotted animals so Jacob couldn't breed from them.

Jacob tricks his uncle

Genesis 30:37-43

Laban thought he was very clever. But God blessed Jacob so that he was cleverer still. He found a way to breed the sheep and goats so that soon there were black and white animals wherever he looked! Then Jacob collected his wives, his children, and all his animals—and crept away secretly.

Friends and brothers

Genesis 32:24-32—33:1-17

Jacob had not seen Esau since he left home many years before. He was worried there might be trouble! Then one night Jacob found himself wrestling in the darkness with a stranger. Jacob knew that he had met God—and God had blessed him. When Jacob and Esau met, they were happy to see each other. Esau had forgiven him.

Jacob's favorite son

Genesis 37:3-4

Rachel, Jacob's wife, had died giving birth to baby Benjamin. Joseph was her first-born child and of all Jacob's children, Joseph was his favorite. Jacob gave Joseph a beautiful colored coat to show how much he loved him. But Jacob had other sons—and this gift made them jealous and angry.

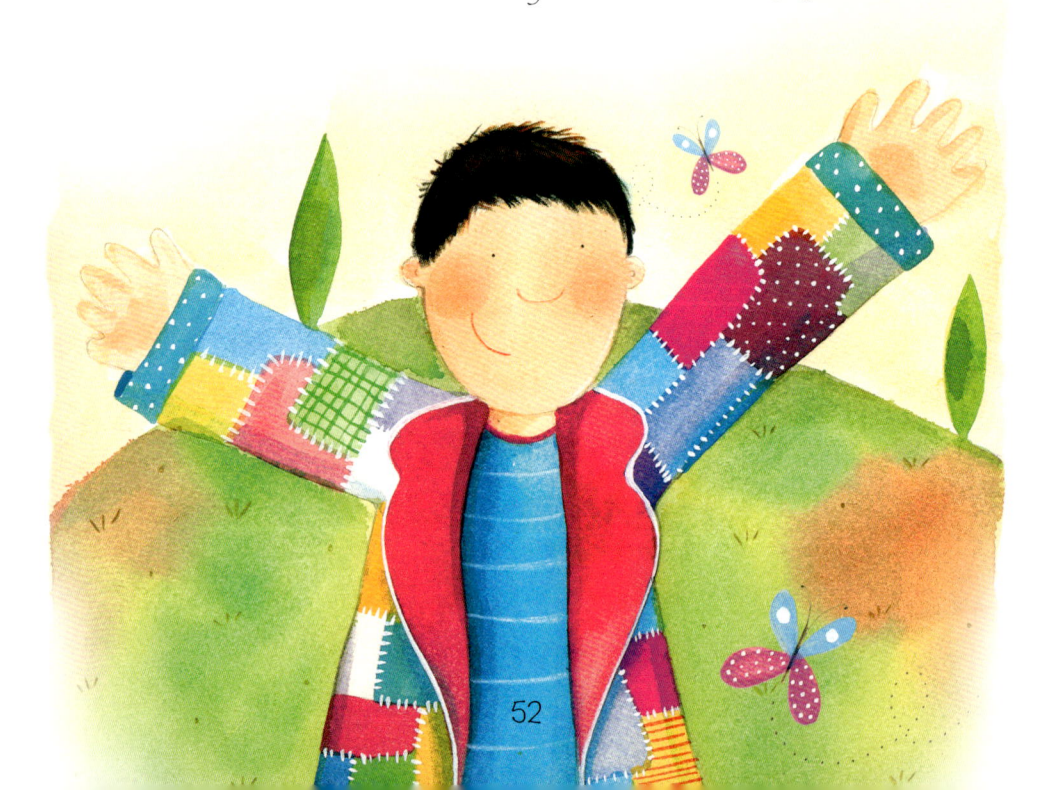

Joseph, the dreamer

Genesis 37:5-11

Joseph dreamed one night that he and his brothers were tying bundles of grain. Joseph's bundle stood up tall—while their bundles bowed down low. Then Joseph dreamed that the sun, moon, and eleven stars bowed down to him. Joseph told his family about his dreams. It looked as if one day the whole family would treat Joseph as a king.

The plot begins
Genesis 37:12-19

Joseph often stayed at home while his brothers took care of his father's sheep and goats. One day, Jacob sent Joseph to see them on a hillside a long way off— they had been gone for a long time. Joseph set off cheerfully on his journey. But when the brothers saw Joseph coming, they began to grumble about him.

Things go wrong for Joseph
Genesis 37:20-24

By the time Joseph had reached his brothers, they had decided that the family would be happier without him there. They were ready for a fight. Most of them wanted to kill Joseph! They ripped off his beautiful coat and threw him into a nearby hole in the ground while they thought about what to do.

The long walk to Egypt

Genesis 37:25-35

While they were thinking, some spice traders on camels passed by. The traders agreed to pay twenty silver coins if they could take Joseph to Egypt to be sold as a slave. The brothers dipped Joseph's coat in goat's blood and told Jacob that their little brother had been killed by a wild animal.

Sold as a slave to Potiphar

Genesis 39:1-5

Joseph could not understand how all these bad things had happened to him. But Potiphar was a kind master. When Joseph became a slave in his house, Potiphar saw that he worked hard and he was good to him. God had not forgotten Joseph. God blessed everything that he did.

Things go wrong again...
Genesis 39:6-20

Potiphar's wife saw that Joseph was a handsome young man. Day by day she would follow him around the house and try to persuade him to kiss her! Joseph knew it would be wrong to kiss his master's wife, so he kept away from her. This made Potiphar's wife angry, so she told her husband lies about Joseph. And Joseph was thrown into a prison cell.

Dreams and more dreams

Genesis 40:1-22

Joseph was joined in prison by the king's butler and baker. Soon they were asking Joseph to help them. They had dreamed strange dreams… Joseph had good news for the butler. Joseph told him his dream meant that he would work for the king again in three days. But Joseph turned sadly to the baker: in three days, he would be hanged… It all happened just as Joseph had said.

Two years later...

Genesis 41:1-8

When the butler was released from prison, he promised to tell the king that Joseph had been innocent and should not be in prison at all. But the butler forgot all about Joseph—until the king himself had strange dreams about ears of corn and fat cows being eaten by thin, bony cows. Suddenly the butler thought of Joseph!

God's warning

Genesis 41:9-28

"I know someone who can help you!" the butler told the king. "There's an Israelite in your prison who understands what dreams mean…" So Joseph was brought from his prison cell and washed and shaved. Then the king told Joseph all about his strange dreams. "Only God can help you," said Joseph. "He is sending you a warning."

Good harvests and bad

Genesis 41:29-49, 53-57

Joseph told the king that there would be seven years of harvests that would fill their barns to overflowing! But then there would be seven years of terrible famine. The king needed a man to store the grain so no one would go hungry… The king knew that Joseph should be that man! So Joseph went from a slave in prison to the most powerful man in Egypt next to the king.

Famine in Israel

Genesis 42:1-3

Soon Joseph was wearing fine clothes and jewelry. He rode around in his own chariot. Everything happened as he said it would. When famine came, he opened the storehouses of grain and made sure everyone had enough to eat. But in Israel, Joseph's family was hungry. So Jacob sent ten of his sons to Egypt to buy food.

Ten men from Canaan

Genesis 42:5-8

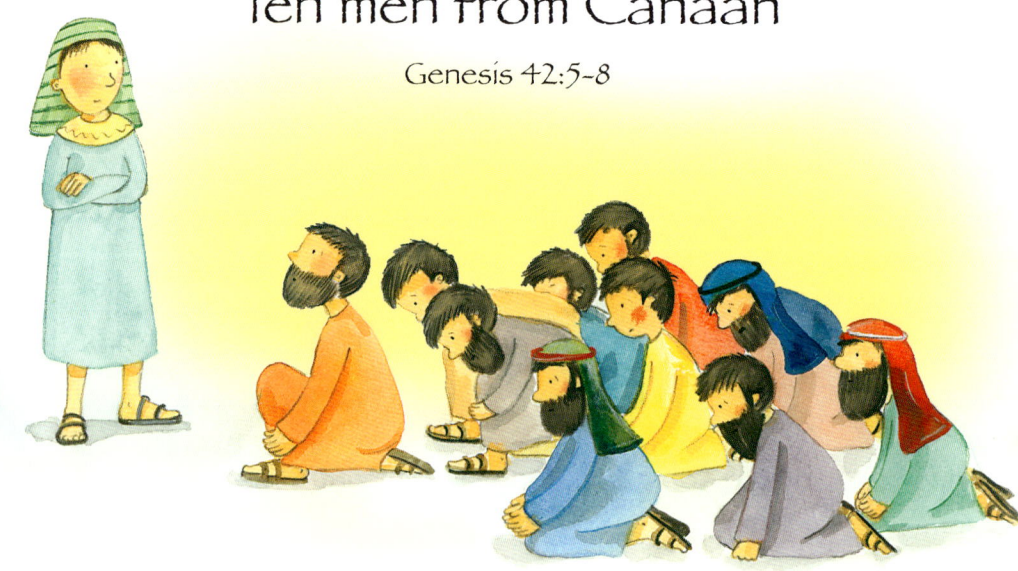

When Joseph's brothers bowed low before the man in charge of all the grain in Egypt, they did not recognize him as their long-lost brother. But Joseph knew who they were! He realized that the dreams he had dreamed all those years ago had come true. Joseph pretended he didn't understand their language. He decided to test them.

Sacks of grain

Genesis 42:11-38

Joseph was very happy to see his brothers—but he wanted to know if they were sorry for what they had done to him. "Prove you are not spies!" Joseph said to them. "Bring your brother Benjamin here—and one of you must stay behind as a hostage." Then Joseph sent them home to Canaan with sacks full of grain.

Joseph's silver cup
Genesis 43:1—44:11

When the sacks were empty, Benjamin went with his brothers back to Egypt. Jacob was very sad to see them go... Joseph treated them kindly but when he sent them home with more sacks of grain, he also hid his special silver cup in Benjamin's sack. Just as the brothers were leaving, a servant stopped them. "Stop! Someone has stolen my master's silver cup!"

Joseph weeps for joy

Genesis 44:12—45:15

The brothers could not believe it when the cup was found in Benjamin's sack. "Punish me, not Benjamin!" they said. So Joseph knew that his brothers had changed. He threw his arms around them and told them who he was. "God has taken care of all of us," he said. "I couldn't have helped you in the famine if I had not been here in Egypt."

Jacob's blessing

Genesis 45:25-28; 47:5-12; 48:1-21

When Jacob heard that Joseph was alive after all this time, he could not wait to see him. The king told Joseph to bring his whole family to Egypt to live. At last they were together again. Jacob grew old in Egypt and asked God to bless Joseph's sons before he died. "God will take you home to Canaan one day," he said.

Joseph dies in Egypt
Genesis 50:22-26

Joseph lived a long time in the land of Egypt. His sons grew up and had children and grandchildren of their own. God had blessed them all and kept them safe. But as time passed, the land of Egypt became full of Joseph's family and their descendants. The time would soon come when they would not be welcome in Egypt any more.

Slaves in Egypt

Exodus 1:1-14

A new king ruled Egypt. He did not care what Joseph had done for his people long ago. He saw that his land was full of Israelites—and he was afraid. So the new king made them all his slaves. They worked hard in the hot sun and he beat them to make them work harder. But still their numbers grew.

The baby in the basket

Exodus 1:22—2:4

The king ordered his soldiers to throw every Israelite baby boy into the River Nile! So a woman hid her infant son from the soldiers for as long as she could. Then she asked God to look after him and her daughter, Miriam, to watch over him. She put him in a basket by the river bank.

Moses and the princess
Exodus 2:5-10

Soon one of the king's daughters came down to the river with her maids. "Fetch me that basket," she said. Then she saw the little baby inside. "Poor little boy," she said. "I will keep him and call him Moses." Miriam came out of her hiding place. "Shall I find someone to care for him?" she asked. So Miriam fetched her mother, who looked after Moses until he was old enough to live with the princess.

Moses runs away

Exodus 2:11-15

Moses grew up in the palace like any Egyptian prince. But Moses knew he was an Israelite. When he saw a slave driver beating an Israelite slave, Moses was so angry that he killed the Egyptian and hid his body. But Moses was so afraid that the king would find out that he ran away into the desert.

From prince to shepherd

Exodus 2:16-25

In the desert land of Midian, Moses met seven daughters fetching water from a well. He helped the girls and was brought home to meet their father. Eventually Moses married one of the daughters and made his home in Midian, working for his father-in-law as a shepherd.

The burning bush

Exodus 3:1-10

Year after year, Moses watched over his sheep in the desert. Nothing changed very much around him. Then one day Moses saw a bush that was on fire but did not burn up. "Moses!" It was God's voice speaking to him from the bush. "My people are slaves in Egypt. They pray to me daily to help them. I want you to tell the king to let my people go."

"Let my people go!"
Exodus 4:10-20; 7:1-13

Moses was afraid. "Take your brother, Aaron, with you," said God. "I will help you both." So Moses and Aaron gave the message to the king. "The God of the Israelites, the God of all the world, says, 'Let my people go!'" But the king said, "No! I don't know your God. Why should I do what he says?"

The first plague
Exodus 7:14-24

"Then God will send plagues to the land of Egypt," said Moses. Aaron touched the green water of the River Nile with his stick and suddenly, the water turned blood red. "Let my people go!" God said again. The king said, "Yes!" but as soon as God made the water clean again, the king changed his mind.

The plague of frogs
Exodus 8:1-15

So God sent a second plague. Aaron stretched out his hand over the River Nile and suddenly there were frogs everywhere. There were frogs in the houses and frogs in the palace. There were frogs in the ovens and frogs in the beds. "Let my people go!" said God. The king said, "Yes!" but as soon as the frogs died, the king changed his mind.

The plagues of gnats and flies
Exodus 8:16-32

So God sent more plagues. The dust gathered into a big cloud of tiny gnats that bit everyone from head to toe. Then God sent a swarm of flies that covered the Egyptians but didn't touch God's people. "Let my people go!" said God. As before, the king said, "Yes!" but as soon as God took away the gnats and the flies, the king changed his mind.

A terrible time in Egypt
Exodus 9:1-17

So God sent more plagues. Now all of the Egyptian livestock became ill and died while God kept the animals of the Israelites safe. When the king still would not let his people go, God sent red, itchy boils to plague the Egyptians. "Let my people go!" said God. The king said, "Yes!" but then he changed his mind.

The plague of hailstones

Exodus 9:18-35

So God sent a seventh plague. A hailstorm beat down upon the land of Egypt. Sharp pieces of ice destroyed the plants so that fields of crops were ruined. God sent down thunder, hail, and fire. "Let my people go!" said God. The king said, "Yes!" but then he changed his mind.

The eighth and ninth plagues
Exodus 10:1-29

So God sent more plagues. An east wind blew locusts all over the land. They stripped the fields of anything the hail had not already destroyed. "Listen to God!" begged the king's servants, but he refused to give in. Then Moses stretched out his hand. God brought darkness on the land for three whole days. "Let my people go!" said God. The king said, "Yes!" but then he changed his mind.

The final plague

Exodus 11:1-10

"Never come here to see me again!" the king said to Moses. "If you do, you will die!" So God told Moses about the last terrible plague. That night, at midnight, all the first-born males in Egypt would die. It was just like the time when Moses was born and the king had tried to drown all the baby boys. Moses told God's people to ask the Egyptians for silver and gold and to prepare for a long journey.

The Passover

Exodus 12:1-13

God said to Moses, "Tell my people to eat their last meal in Egypt and be dressed and ready for a journey. They must roast a lamb with bitter herbs and eat it with bread made without yeast. They must mark their doors with the blood of the lamb so that the angel of death will pass over them." That night the Israelites heard wailing in every Egyptian home.

The king says, "Go!"
Exodus 12:29-41

The king of Egypt held his dead son in his arms with tears running down his cheeks. He called for Moses and Aaron. "Take your people and go!" he said. So Moses gathered all the Israelites. Thousands of men, women, and children started the journey out of Egypt that night. They took with them everything they owned and all the silver and gold the Egyptians had given them.

God leads his people
Exodus 13:17-22

Moses told the people that God would lead them out of Egypt and out of slavery. God made a pillar of cloud for all the Israelites to follow during the day. At night, God led them with a pillar of bright fire that shone in the darkness. Everyone could see the cloud and the fire—even those who were right at the back. It was a journey they would never forget.

Crossing the Red Sea
Exodus 14:1-28

Then the king changed his mind again… He sent his army of chariots after the Israelites. Soon the Israelites were trapped—between the king's army and the Red Sea. Moses held out his stick and the sea parted so that the Israelites walked safely across to the other side. Then Moses raised his stick again and the water washed over the chariots of the Egyptians who were following.

Learning to trust God
Exodus 15:22-27

The Israelites were no longer slaves. They thanked God for saving them and celebrated their escape to freedom. But now they were on a new journey to the land of Canaan. It wasn't long before they were tired and thirsty. "Trust God! He will give us everything we need," said Moses. God led them to an oasis where there were palm trees with sweet dates to eat and springs of fresh water.

Food in the desert

Exodus 16:1-21

The Israelites were happy for only a little while before they started to grumble again. "At least we had good food to eat when we were slaves in Egypt," they complained. God blessed them with quails to eat in the evenings and manna that tasted of honey in the mornings.

Mountaintop experience
Exodus 19:1-25

The Israelites walked through the desert until they reached the foot of Mount Sinai. Then Moses went up the mountain to meet with God. Thunder and lightning crashed, and a very loud trumpet sounded. And while the people waited, God spoke to Moses. God gave Moses laws to help his people live together in peace.

The Ten Commandments

Exodus 20:2-17

"God is the only God. Don't worship anything else. Respect God's holy name. Keep the Sabbath as a special day. Love and respect your parents. Don't murder. Don't steal anyone's wife or husband. Don't steal anything. Don't tell lies about people and don't be jealous of things other people have."

Down the mountain

Exodus 31:18

God gave these special rules to Moses on two large pieces of stone. Afterwards they were known as the Ten Commandments. Moses spent a long time on the mountain talking with God. While he was away, the people were anxious. They wondered what was happening. When Moses came down again, he saw something that made him very sad.

The golden calf

Exodus 32:1-19

The Israelites wanted a god they could see. So they had asked Aaron to make them a god like the ones they had known back home. Aaron made a golden calf from the people's golden rings and jewelry and when Moses came down the mountain, Moses saw that they were worshiping it.

Moses prays for God's people
Exodus 32:20-35

Moses knew that God was the only true and living God. Moses had seen him and heard him! But the people were weak. "Forgive them," Moses prayed. "They need to learn to trust You. Lord, You loved and cared for Abraham, Isaac, and Jacob. Don't be angry with Your people now." Then Moses asked the people to follow him—if they wanted to love God.

Priests and helpers

Numbers 17—18

Some of the people followed Moses. Then God chose priests from the descendants of Jacob's son, Levi. The priests would teach them the Ten Commandments and help them when they made mistakes or did bad things. The priests would help God's people worship Him.

A special agreement
Exodus 25:10-22

The Ten Commandments were an agreement or covenant between God and his people. The people would follow the rules and God would take care of them. The Commandments were kept in a box called the ark of the covenant. It was trimmed with gold and had gold rings on each side so it could be carried on poles wherever the Israelites went.

Twelve spies

Numbers 13: 1-25

God's people spent many years in the desert before they reached the land that God had promised to them. Then Moses sent twelve spies into Canaan to find out what the land and its people were like, one spy from each of the tribes descended from Jacob. Was the land good to grow food? Were the people friendly?

The spies' report
Numbers 13:26—14:4

Ten of the spies came back with stories about the fierce and unfriendly people of Canaan! Joshua and Caleb had a different report. They told everyone that God had led them to a beautiful land with fresh water and plump fruit and vegetables to eat. But the Israelites were afraid. They decided not to live in Canaan. They did not trust God to look after them.

Joshua, the new leader

Deuteronomy 34:1-7; Joshua 1:1-9

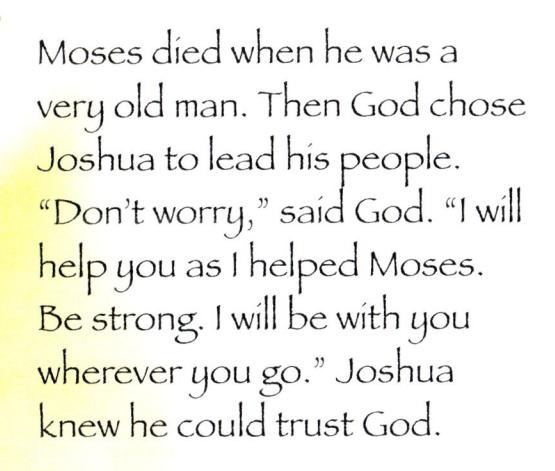

Moses died when he was a very old man. Then God chose Joshua to lead his people. "Don't worry," said God. "I will help you as I helped Moses. Be strong. I will be with you wherever you go." Joshua knew he could trust God.

Spies in Jericho!

Joshua 2:1-13

The walled city of Jericho stood between God's people and the land of Canaan. So Joshua sent two men to find out about the people there. A woman called Rahab lived in a house built into the city wall. "Everyone knows how your God led you out of Egypt," she told them. "We know God will give you the land of Canaan. So please—be kind to my family when you take the city."

A narrow escape
Joshua 2:14-21

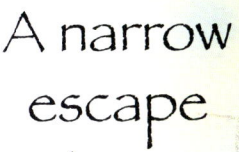

Rahab knew the king was looking for the spies. She hid them under some flax on her roof until it was safe to let them escape through her window. The spies promised that her family would not be harmed as long as she marked her window with a red ribbon.

The fast-flowing river

Joshua 3:1-13

The Israelites had camped on one side of the River Jordan, which was full and overflowing its banks. Joshua prepared them for the battle ahead and the miracle that God had promised him. But first, everyone had to cross the river—and there were thousands of people.

A safe crossing

Joshua 3:14—4:24

The priests walked into the river first carrying the Ten Commandments. The river stopped flowing as soon as their feet touched the water. Then all the people crossed over safely on dry ground. Joshua chose a man from each of the twelve tribes to bring a stone from the river bed to mark the place where God had brought them into Canaan.

The city of Jericho
Joshua 6:1-14

Now the fortress city of Jericho with its strong, high walls was in front of them. "Don't be afraid," said God. "I am here to help you." Then he gave Joshua a strange plan. The Israelites had to march around the city every day for six days, while seven priests blew on their trumpets.

Walls come tumbling down

Joshua 6:15-25

On the seventh day, the Israelites marched around the city seven more times. The last time around Joshua commanded everyone to shout with all their might! And the walls of Jericho came tumbling down. The city was theirs. Rahab and her family joined the Israelites and were happy to be part of God's people.

The land of Canaan

Judges 2:10

When Joshua died, the people settled in Canaan. It was a good place to be and they were happy. The nation grew so that the promise God made to Abraham came true—he had as many descendants as stars in the sky. God was blessing them. They had only to remember to keep God's commandments.

Broken promises

Judges 2:11—3:8

But the Israelites did not remember. They did not keep God's commandments. They worshiped false gods. They were cruel to each other. They had broken their promises. Then God stopped protecting them from their enemies and they became slaves again, just as their ancestors had been slaves in Egypt.

A prophet called Deborah

Judges 4:4-8

God's people realized that they needed His help. So they went to Deborah who still heard God's voice. God told Deborah how she could help them. "God wants you to fight against Sisera," she told a soldier named Barak one day. "Me?" he replied. "But I can't!" Barak was scared. Sisera was the cruel Canaanite general.

A brave woman's victory

Judges 4:9-24

"God will help you," Deborah told him, "but because you do not trust him, he will give the victory to a woman, not to you." The battle was a fierce one. But God sent rain and Sisera's chariots got stuck in the mud. Sisera ran away and hid in the tent of a woman called Jael. While Sisera was sleeping, Jael used a tent peg to kill him.

God chooses Gideon

Judges 6:11-17

"God has chosen you, Gideon!" said an angel one day. "He wants you to save his people from the Midianites." God's people needed to be saved. The Midianites had been raiding their crops—and the people were frightened and hungry. But Gideon was afraid. "Please give me a sign," he said.

A sign for Gideon

Judges 6:36-40

Gideon asked God to make a fleece wet with dew when the ground was dry. And God did. But Gideon was not convinced. Now he asked God to make the fleece dry while the ground was wet with dew. And God did. Gideon was not a soldier—but now he believed that God would help him.

A very small army
Judges 7:1-8

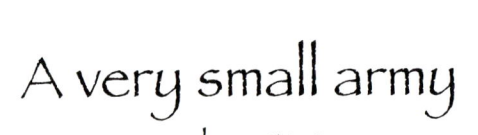

Gideon gathered 30,000 men to be part of God's army. But God told Gideon to send away anyone who was afraid. Lots of men went home! Gideon then asked the men who were left to go down to drink from the river. God told Gideon to take with him only the men who scooped up the water with their hands. Now Gideon had only 300 men left.

A victory for God
Judges 7:15-24

Gideon gave each man a trumpet and a flaming torch inside a jar. The Israelites went by night to the camp of the Midianites and surrounded them. Then they blew their trumpets, broke the jars so the light shone out, and shouted! The Midianites woke up and ran in fear for their lives. It was a victory! The Israelites were free again.

Naomi's sadness

Ruth 1:1-18

Naomi's husband and two grown-up sons
had died in Moab. Naomi was very sad.
She decided to go home to Bethlehem.
"I have nothing left to give you," she told
her sons' wives. "Go back to your mothers."
Orpah went home. But Ruth would not go.
"I am your daughter now. I will go with
you and look after you. And I will worship
your God," she said.

Ruth's kindness

Ruth 2:1-3

Naomi was welcomed in Bethlehem. People were sorry that her family had died. But they also smiled at Ruth. They saw that she was good and kind. Soon Ruth was gathering barley in the fields of a man called Boaz so that she and Naomi would have enough to eat.

Ruth meets Boaz

Ruth 2:4-12

Poor people were allowed to pick up the barley left behind after the fields had been harvested. "Gather as much as you need," Boaz said to Ruth. But when Naomi saw how much grain Ruth had collected, she knew that Boaz had asked his workers to help Ruth. Boaz was a kind man.

Naomi's little grandson
Ruth 4:9-17

Boaz saw that Ruth was a good daughter to Naomi. He saw that she was kind and loyal. Soon they became friends and Boaz married Ruth. Naomi had been so sad, but now she had a daughter and a son-in-law to take care of her. She soon became a grandmother, too, when Ruth gave birth to a baby boy. They called him Obed.

Hannah's prayer
1 Samuel 1:1-28

Hannah loved her husband, but although everyone she knew had babies, Hannah had no child of her own. She prayed for God to bless her with a baby son. She told God that she would let her son grow up in the temple and serve God there. Hannah was very happy when God answered her prayer! She called her son Samuel.

God calls Samuel

1 Samuel 3:1-9

When he was older, Samuel went to the temple where Eli, the priest, taught him how to love God. One night, Samuel heard someone call him. "Here I am!" he said to Eli. But Eli sent him back to bed. "I didn't call you," he said. It happened a second and then a third time. Then Eli said, "God is speaking to you, Samuel. Listen to God, and do all he tells you."

Samuel, prophet and judge
1 Samuel 7:1-14

Eli realized that God had chosen Samuel to be the next prophet. Samuel would help his people defeat their enemy. "Stop worshiping false gods," Samuel told them. "Love God—then he will rescue you from the Philistines." Samuel prayed for the Israelites. When the Philistines attacked them, God sent a storm to confuse the attackers. Then for a while there was peace in the land.

Israel wants a king
1 Samuel 8:4-22

Samuel was a good prophet and a wise judge. But when he was an old man, the people were worried about what would happen when he died. "Give us a king so we can be like all the other nations," they said. "But God will look after you," Samuel told them. "God is your king." But the people wanted a king they could see.

Wandering donkeys
1 Samuel 9:1-10

God told Samuel that the people could have what they asked for. God would send the young man who would be king to find him. Then God sent a man named Saul to look for some donkeys that had wandered off. Saul and his servant walked for miles before spotting Samuel. They approached Samuel to ask if he had seen their donkeys.

The first king of Israel

1 Samuel 9:17—10:1

Samuel saw the tall, handsome man coming toward him. "Here he is," said God. "This is the man you must anoint as king." Samuel welcomed Saul and his servant—and told them that the lost donkeys had been found. "I have important news for you," Samuel told Saul. "God wants me to anoint you king of Israel."

The people's king
1 Samuel 10:17-24

Saul was nervous about Samuel's news. He knew he was not clever or important. Why would God choose him? So when Samuel announced to the twelve tribes of Israel that they finally had a king they could see, Saul was hiding among all the bags. Samuel brought him out—and the people cheered, "Long live the king!"

Things go wrong
1 Samuel 15:1-35

God helped Saul to be a good king, and everyone was happy when he led the people to defeat their enemies. But King Saul liked to do things his own way. Soon he stopped listening to God. He thought he knew best. Things began to go wrong. Then Samuel wept. God had rejected Saul as king.

Seven handsome sons

1 Samuel 16:1-10

"Go to visit Jesse," God told Samuel. "It's time to choose a new king." Jesse introduced seven of his sons to Samuel. They were all tall and strong. "Looks are not everything," said God. "I can see what people are like inside—and we want someone good and kind and wise." God did not choose any of Jesse's seven sons.

The eighth son of Jesse

1 Samuel 16:11-12

"Have you any more sons?" Samuel asked. "My youngest son is called David," Jesse replied. "He takes care of my sheep—but I will send someone to fetch him." When David arrived, God told Samuel to anoint him as king. "This is the next king of Israel," said God.

Music for King Saul

1 Samuel 16:14-18

King Saul was grumpy and moody. He shouted at his servants. He frowned all the time. Nothing seemed right anymore. "Perhaps we could get someone to play the harp for you," said one of his servants. "It may help you to sleep." So they found a shepherd boy who loved God and wrote songs. His name was David.

The shepherd's song
Psalm 23

David came to play his harp for the king. Saul liked his music so much that he wanted him to be at court whenever he needed him. "God is my shepherd," sang David. "He gives me everything I need. He leads me to quiet places. Nothing can frighten me, because God is always there to help me."

Goliath the champion
1 Samuel 17:1-11

The Israelites had an enemy at their border. The Philistines were big and strong and were always challenging Israelites to fight. Even King Saul was afraid of Goliath, their champion. Goliath was over nine feet tall! But when David heard Goliath's challenge, he was very angry. He knew that God was stronger than a Philistine!

Bears and lions

1 Samuel 17:32-39

"I will fight Goliath," said David. King Saul was worried. Saul made David put on his own armor. But the helmet fell over his eyes. Everything was too big and too heavy. David took it off. "When I took care of my sheep, God protected me from lions and bears," David said. "God will help me now."

David fights the giant

1 Samuel 17:45-50

"You may be big and strong," said David. "You may even have better armor. But the God of all the world is here to help me." Then David slung a smooth stone from his slingshot—and hit Goliath in the forehead. The giant fell down, dead.

David and Jonathan

1 Samuel 18:1-15; 19:1-2

David became famous. At first Saul was pleased to have such a brave young man working for him. David and Saul's son, Jonathan, became best friends. But when Saul saw how all the people loved David, he was jealous. Jonathan warned David that Saul wanted to kill him! Saul became David's enemy. But when King Saul died, the people wanted David to be their king.

King David

2 Samuel 6:12-19

When David became king, there was peace in the land of Israel. They had a king who loved God and everyone was happy. David had been born in Bethlehem but he made the city of Jerusalem his home. He celebrated when he brought the ark of the covenant to Jerusalem.

David's big temptation
2 Samuel 11:2-3

David was married. But one day, while his army was away at war, he saw a very beautiful woman. David couldn't stop thinking about her. He decided that he wanted her to be his wife, too. David found out that the woman's name was Bathsheba. She already had a husband, Uriah, a soldier in his army.

David's big mistake
2 Samuel 11:14-26

Then David did a terrible thing. He asked Joab, his commander, to move Uriah to the place where the battle was the most dangerous. He arranged for Uriah to be killed. When the news reached him that Uriah was dead, David was pleased. Now Bathsheba was free to become his wife.

The prophet, Nathan

2 Samuel 11:27 — 12:6

David and Bathsheba had a baby son. Everything seemed to be fine. But God was very angry with David. God sent Nathan to tell David a story. Nathan told David about a rich man who had many sheep of his own   but he stole a poor man's only lamb and killed it. "The rich man deserves to die!" David said.

David weeps

2 Samuel 12:7-13

"You are right," said Nathan. "He has done a terrible thing—just like the terrible thing you have done. You, a king with many wives, stole Uriah's precious wife and then killed him! Has God not given you enough good things?" Then David put his head in his hands. "I have sinned," he said. "I am so very sorry."

God blesses David

2 Samuel 12:14-25

God forgave David. But when Bathsheba's baby son became ill and died, David was sure it was his fault. He was very unhappy. After a while God blessed David and Bathsheba with another son. They called him Solomon. David wanted Solomon to be king when he died.

David's son, Absalom

2 Samuel 13—18

David also loved his son Absalom. But Absalom wanted to be king. David's soldiers were at war with Absalom's friends and followers. One day there was a fierce battle. Absalom was riding through the forest when his long hair got stuck in a tree. While he hung there, some of David's soldiers came and killed him. David was very sad. He had lost another son.

Solomon's dream

1 Kings 3:5-15

Before he died, David told Solomon to keep God's commandments—then he would be a better king than his father had been. After he was anointed king, Solomon dreamed that God asked him what gift he would like. "I am still very young," Solomon said. "Please make me wise so I can be a good king." God made Solomon wise, rich, and famous!

Wise King Solomon
1 Kings 3:16-28

Two women came to see King Solomon. "She stole my baby!" said one. "No, her baby died!" said the other. "Cut the baby in half," Solomon said. One of the women said, "Yes!" The other said, "No!" Solomon knew the real mother would protect her baby. He gave the child to the second woman. Everyone saw that God had made Solomon wise.

Solomon's temple

1 Kings 5:13—6:38

Solomon wanted to build a temple so the people could worship God in Jerusalem. The temple was made with stone walls paneled with wood and covered in gold. It was decorated with carved flowers and golden angels. It took seven years to finish the temple even though thousands of men worked hard to make it strong and beautiful.

God's house

1 Kings 8:22-66

The priests carried the ark of the covenant into the temple. "I know You are a great God and You do not live in houses made by men," Solomon prayed. "But let Your people worship You here. Hear the prayers Your people pray here. Listen when they tell You they are sorry and forgive them when they do things that are wrong."

The queen of Sheba

1 Kings 10:1-13

Far away in the land of Sheba, the queen heard about Solomon. She traveled to Israel to find out whether he was really wise and good. "God has truly blessed you," she told him when she had seen his palace and heard the things he said. She offered Solomon gifts of gold, precious stones, and spices.

A bad king and a wicked queen

1 Kings 16:29-33

King Ahab did not love God as David and Solomon had. Ahab broke all God's rules. He married a foreign woman called Jezebel and set up an altar to Baal, the pretend god she worshiped. Ahab thanked a pretend god for watering the land and giving good harvests. And what the king of Israel did, the people of Israel followed.

No more rain

1 Kings 17:1

Elijah was one of God's prophets. "Our God is the only true and living God," Elijah told King Ahab. "Only He can water the land and give good harvests. You should be worshiping Him. And until you do, God will send no more rain. There will be a terrible drought." Elijah's message made King Ahab very angry.

God takes care of Elijah

1 Kings 17:2-6

Elijah did not wait to see what would happen next. God sent him to a place east of the River Jordan. There Elijah found a brook with clear running water that he could drink. Each morning God sent ravens with food for Elijah's breakfast and each evening the ravens brought him his supper. The sun was hot. There was still no rain.

The oil that never ran out

1 Kings 17:7-16

"Go now to Zarephath," God told Elijah. There Elijah met a woman gathering sticks for her fire. "Do you have some bread you could give me?" Elijah asked. "This is all we have left," the woman told him. "Share it with me," Elijah said. "God has promised that you will have enough oil and flour to make more." The woman shared with Elijah. After that her flour and oil did not run out until it rained again.

Time to choose

1 Kings 18:16-19

Three years had passed. The land was dry and parched. It was time to see King Ahab again. "Are you ready to tell God you are sorry?" asked Elijah. "Will you stop worshiping Baal and love God instead? Gather everyone on Mount Carmel. It is time to choose who the real God is—and then follow Him!"

The prophets of Baal
1 Kings 18:20-29

Elijah challenged the prophets of Baal to call on their god to bring down fire on an altar. He would do the same. The people watched as the prophets danced and shouted and shouted and danced. Nothing happened; nothing at all. "Is your god asleep?" asked Elijah. "Has he gone away on vacation?"

Elijah's prayer
1 Kings 18:30-37

Then it was Elijah's turn. He built an altar of twelve stones with a small trench around it. He told the people to pour water all over everything until there was a small river around a very wet altar. Surely nothing could burn on that! Then, while all the people watched him, Elijah prayed. "Lord, show everyone here that you alone are the true and living God."

Fire and rain

1 Kings 18:38-46

God answered Elijah's prayer. Fire fell from heaven! It burned up everything on Elijah's altar. It even dried up all the water in the trench. The people saw that God was real. They knew that He alone should be worshiped — and they knelt down before Him. Then the God of all the earth sent rain at once. The drought was over.

Jezebel's threats

1 Kings 19:1-12

Jezebel was very angry with Elijah. So Elijah ran for his life! Soon Elijah realized that he was lonely and afraid. God comforted him, sending an angel to him with food and water. But still Elijah was sad. Then God told Elijah to meet Him on the mountain. Elijah waited. First there was a roaring wind around him. Then there was an earthquake followed by fire. But when God came, it was with a gentle whisper.

Chariot of fire

2 Kings 2:1-11

It was time for Elijah to finish his work on earth. God told him to find Elisha, who would be the prophet to follow him. Elisha went with Elijah to the River Jordan, where the water divided for them to cross on dry land. Then Elisha watched as a chariot of fire, drawn by horses, carried Elijah away to heaven to be with God.

The little servant girl

2 Kings 5:1-7

Naaman had leprosy. The little Israelite girl who worked for him persuaded him to go to Israel and ask Elisha for help. But Naaman was the proud captain of the Aramean army. First he wanted to go to the King of Israel. "How can I help him?" shouted the king. He was afraid Naaman's request was an excuse to declare war on him!

God heals Naaman

2 Kings 5:8-14

Elisha told the king that God could heal Naaman. He sent a message telling Naaman to wash seven times in the River Jordan, then he would be healed. Naaman was proud and angry. There were better rivers in his own land! But he washed in the River Jordan just the same—and his skin became as clear and new as a baby's. God had healed him, thanks to the little servant girl.

Jonah is sent to Nineveh

Jonah 1:1-2

The Assyrians had been enemies of God's people for a long time. They were cruel and greedy. So when God told Jonah to go to Nineveh and warn the people to change their ways, Jonah didn't want to go! He knew what God was like. God was good and kind, loving and forgiving. Maybe He would forgive the people of Nineveh—but they deserved to be punished!

Jonah hides from God

Jonah 1:3-6

So Jonah ran away. He boarded a boat going in the opposite direction, found somewhere below deck to hide away, and fell asleep. Jonah forgot that you can't hide from God. Suddenly a massive storm rocked the boat. The sailors threw the cargo overboard. Then they woke Jonah.
"Pray to your God!" they shouted.

Swallowed by a big fish
Jonah 1:7—2:1

Jonah knew that the storm was his fault. "Throw me overboard! Then God will save you," Jonah told them. "This is all because of me!" So the sailors threw Jonah over the side. Down, down he plunged into the sea. Then God sent a great fish to swallow him up. Jonah sat for three days and three nights in the body of the fish and prayed to God.

God forgives

Jonah 2:10— 3:10

"I'm sorry," Jonah told God. "I will go to Nineveh." So the fish spat Jonah out onto dry land. Jonah then made his way to the great city. He told people that God was angry at their cruelty. He warned them to change their ways… and the people listened. They were sorry. They changed their ways. And Jonah was right about God. He was kind and loving. God forgave the people of Nineveh.

God's plans for Jeremiah

Jeremiah 1:1-10

Jeremiah was a young man when God asked him to be a prophet. "I loved you even before you were born," said God. "I have plans for your future and will help you with everything you need to do." God's people had forgotten His special rules again. They needed His help.

The potter and the clay

Jeremiah 18:1-6

Jeremiah watched the potter at work. As the wheel spun around, the clay went wobbly. It made a funny shape. But the potter gently worked the clay until it made a perfect pot. God was like the potter, thought Jeremiah. His people were like the clay. God could change His people into something better even when they had made a mess of things.

A warning for the king

Jeremiah 36:1-25

"You have a God who loves you!" Jeremiah said. "God wants to help you! But you won't listen to Him. You ignore His warnings. Listen now before the king of Babylon comes to attack you." Jeremiah wrote down the warning, but the king burned the words in the open fire.

Babylon—the enemy
Jeremiah 24; 37:1—38:3

So the king of Babylon captured all the skilled men from Jerusalem and took them away to work for him. First one king, then another, was taken captive. All the treasures in the temple were stolen. Jeremiah warned King Zedekiah that he must surrender soon or the people would starve and the city of Jerusalem would be destroyed.

Alone in a dark well

Jeremiah 38:4-6

The king did not like Jeremiah's message. His officials did not like it either—it made everyone nervous and afraid. But they still did not ask God for help. Instead they threw Jeremiah into an empty well and left him there to die.

A friend for Jeremiah

Jeremiah 38:7-16

Someone went to the king and asked him to be kind to Jeremiah. "Don't let Jeremiah die," he said. "Let us help him." So the king allowed the man to set Jeremiah free. But Jeremiah could not change the message God had given him. And the king still refused to listen.

Jerusalem is destroyed

Jeremiah 39:1-9

Then the message God had given to Jeremiah came true. The Babylonians broke through the gates of Jerusalem and set fire to the palace and the houses there. They broke down the city walls. When they found King Zedekiah, they killed his sons, blinded him, and took him away in chains.

Jeremiah stays in Jerusalem
Jeremiah 40:1-6

At first Jeremiah was taken away with the other captives in chains. But the Babylonian king, Nebuchadnezzar, knew about Jeremiah. He asked his guards to be kind to him and let him return to Jerusalem if he wanted to go. Jeremiah decided to take care of the poorer people who were left behind in the broken city. He went back to Jerusalem.

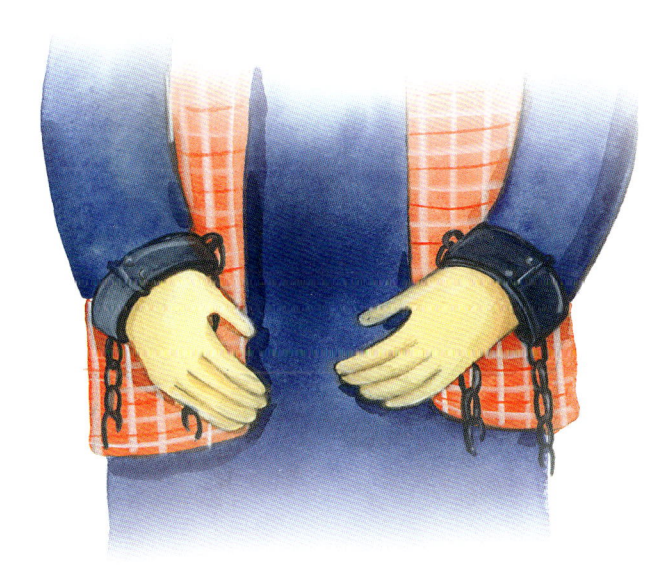

The strange land of Babylon
Daniel 1:1-13

Daniel was among the captives taken to Babylon. They were treated well as long as they would work for King Nebuchadnezzar. "We will work hard," said Daniel, "but please give us only water to drink and vegetables to eat." Daniel did not want to eat food that had been offered to idols. He wanted to keep God's laws in a foreign land.

A very hard task
Daniel 2:1-12

King Nebuchadnezzar called his wise men to him one day. "My dreams keep me awake at night!" he said. "Tell us about them and we will help you," the wise men answered. "No! You tell me what the dreams were or I will have you all killed!" the king replied. Everyone was very afraid. How could anyone do this?

God helps Daniel
Daniel 2:17-30

Daniel and his friends prayed to God to help them. "No one can tell you your dream," Daniel told King Nebuchadnezzar, "except God in heaven. I have asked Him for help and He has answered me. I will tell you your dream and what it means. Then you will know how great God is."

The king's strange dream
Daniel 2:31-45

"You saw a strong statue smashed to pieces by a rock. Then the rock became a great mountain," said Daniel. "The statue is you and your kingdom, great and strong. God is warning you that one day, you will be destroyed. And one day God's kingdom will come and replace all others." King Nebuchadnezzar was amazed.

Daniel's three friends

Daniel 3:1-21

The king soon forgot God's warning. He made a huge golden statue of himself and ordered everyone to bow down and worship it. Shadrach, Meshach, and Abednego would not worship the statue. "We will only worship God," they said. They were thrown into a hot, fiery furnace.

The fiery furnace
Daniel 3:24-29

Shadrach, Meshach, and Abednego did not die. God sent an angel to protect them, so they were not hurt by the flames. When they came out from the fire, they did not even smell of smoke! King Nebuchadnezzar praised their God who had saved them from the fire.

King Belshazzar of Babylon

Daniel 5:1-2

When the king died, his son, Belshazzar, became king. Daniel was an old man now and Belshazzar did not know him. Then one day, Belshazzar threw a big party. He used the beautiful gold and silver goblets that his father had taken from God's temple in Jerusalem. It was a big mistake.

The writing on the wall
Daniel 5:3-7

As King Belshazzar and his guests drank wine from the beautiful goblets, they praised the gods of gold and silver, wood and stone. Then King Belshazzar's face went white. He saw the fingers of a man's hand write on the wall in front of him!

God tests Belshazzar

Daniel 5:13-29

No one knew what the strange message meant. But someone remembered Daniel. He came to help the king. "God has measured your days as king," Daniel explained. "God has tested you, and you have failed. Your kingdom will be given to the Medes and the Persians. Your days as king are over."

Daniel, the governor
Daniel 5:30—6:4

Belshazzar was killed that night; and when Darius the Mede became king, he asked Daniel to help govern his new kingdom. Darius was very pleased with Daniel. But as Daniel was given more power, he also gained some enemies—men who were jealous of him. These men began to look for ways to remove Daniel forever…

Plots against Daniel
Daniel 6:5-15

"King Darius," said Daniel's enemies, "you are so wise and great that people should worship you! Not their Gods or any other person. Anyone who doesn't worship you should be thrown into a den of lions…" King Darius liked this idea so much he made it a law. But Daniel loved God. He would worship only him. So he prayed to God as he did every day. When the men told the king that Daniel had broken his law, Darius knew that he had been tricked. The law could not be changed; Daniel must be thrown to the lions.

In the lions' den

Daniel 6:16-28

Daniel went inside and the door to the lions' den was locked. Next morning, Darius went to find out what had happened. "God sent His angel to shut the lions' mouths," said Daniel. "I am safe!" Then Darius issued a new law. "Everyone should respect Daniel's God, because He alone has the power to save."

Nehemiah wants to go home
Nehemiah 2:1-4

Nehemiah lived in Babylon and was cupbearer to King Artaxerxes. He knew that Jerusalem was still in ruins. It had been many years since the Israelites had lived in Jerusalem together. But Nehemiah prayed that the king would let him go home and rebuild the city's walls and gates.

An answer to prayer
Nehemiah 2:5-20

God answered Nehemiah's prayer. The king not only said Nehemiah could go home, he let him take supplies with him so the rebuilding work could be done. Nehemiah went to Jerusalem and encouraged all the people who lived there. He told them that God would help them start again.

Home at last

Nehemiah 3:1—6:19; 8:1-12

Nehemiah helped the people repair the walls of Jerusalem and build new city gates in just fifty-two days! Then Ezra, the priest, reminded the people about God's promises to them and His special laws given to Moses. The people were very sad when they realized how they had disappointed God, but they thanked God for taking care of them and bringing them home.

God's promised Savior

Malachi 4:4-6

The story did not end when God's people were back in Jerusalem. God told them through the prophet Malachi that soon He would send someone to show them how much He loved them. The people had done many things wrong in the past. Now God would send someone to save them.

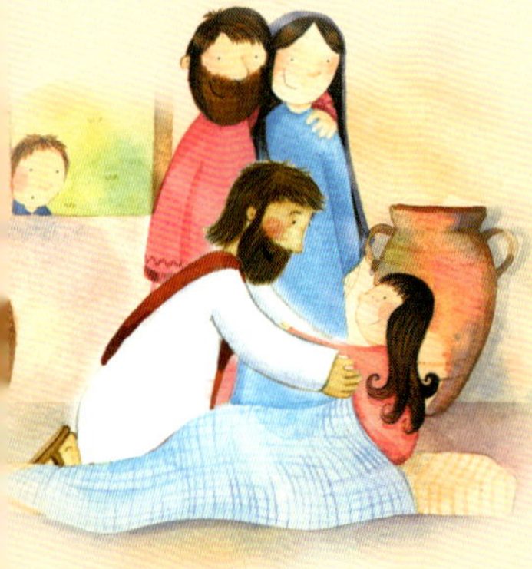
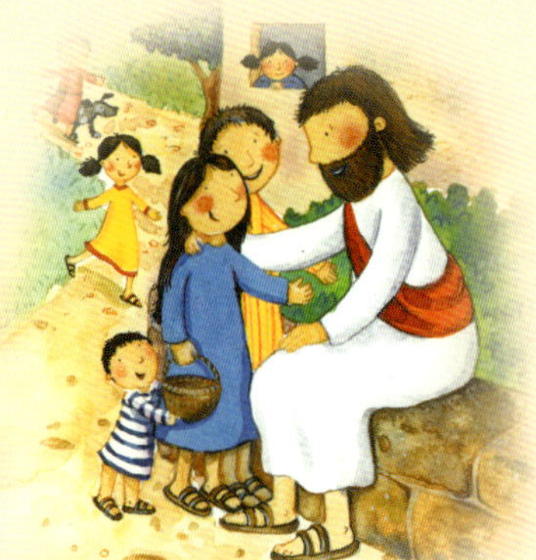
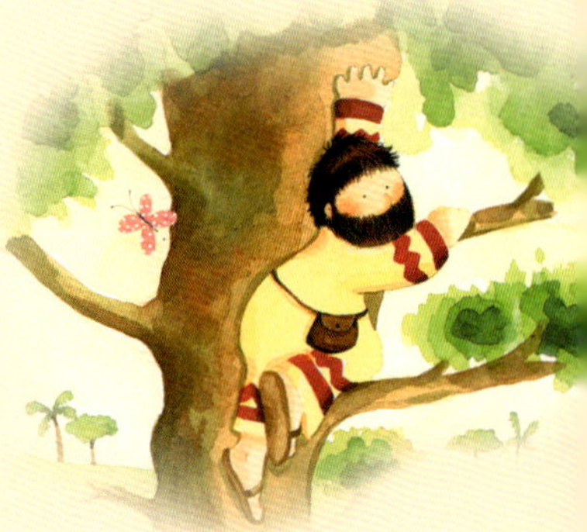

THE NEW TESTAMENT

An angel in the temple
Luke 1:8-17

It was Zechariah's turn to burn the incense in the temple. Suddenly, in the silence, the angel Gabriel spoke to him. "God has heard your prayers, Zechariah. Your wife will have a baby—and you will call him John. He will grow up to be God's special messenger and make everyone ready for the time when God comes to live with his people."

Good news for Elizabeth

Luke 1:18-25

Zechariah was stunned by the news. Surely it was too late for him and his wife to have a child of their own? When he left the temple he could not talk about what he had heard. It would be months before he spoke again. But Elizabeth soon had plenty to talk about. She knew that she was expecting a baby...

Mary's special secret

Luke 1:26-38

The angel Gabriel had to visit Elizabeth's cousin, Mary, some months later. Mary was also surprised by the angel's news. "Don't be afraid, Mary, for God has chosen you to do something very special. You will be the mother of God's Son. You will call him Jesus." Mary was not yet married to Joseph—but she trusted God.

Mary and Elizabeth
Luke 1:39-45

Gabriel had told Mary that Elizabeth was also expecting a baby. So Mary set out to visit her. As soon as Mary arrived, Elizabeth's baby kicked with joy! "God has blessed you, Mary—and I am so lucky that the mother of the promised Savior has come to visit me!" said Elizabeth. "God is great and holy," said Mary. "He has done something very wonderful!"

The Roman census

Luke 2:1-5

God told Joseph to marry Mary and take care of her and her baby. So when Caesar Augustus ordered everyone to return to their family home to be counted, Mary went with Joseph to Bethlehem. Many people were traveling the same way.

No room at the inn

Luke 2:6-7

It was not an easy time for Mary. Joseph found a place for her to rest and that night, Mary's baby boy was born. She called him Jesus, just as the angel had told her. Mary wrapped the baby tightly in clean clothes and made a bed for him in the manger because there was no room for them at the inn.

Shepherds on the hillside

Luke 2:8-12

On the hill outside Bethlehem, shepherds were watching over their sheep. Suddenly the sky was filled with light and they heard the voice of an angel bringing the shepherds good news. "Don't be afraid," said the angel. "Today, your Savior has been born in Bethlehem. You will find him lying in a manger."

Angels in the sky

Luke 2:13-14

Then the shepherds saw hundreds of angels who sang praises to God. It was a wonderful sound! "Glory to God who lives in heaven, and peace to everyone on the earth," the angels sang. The sound echoed around the hillside until the shepherds knew they must go to see the new baby.

The baby in the manger
Luke 2:15-20

The shepherds went to Bethlehem. They knew they had found baby Jesus when they found Mary and Joseph—and a baby, lying in a manger. They praised God for the miracle of his birth. They could not wait to tell everyone they saw what had happened that night!

Wise men in the East

Matthew 2:1

When Jesus was born, a new star appeared in the sky. Wise men in eastern lands saw the star and believed that it was a sign that a new king had been born to the Jewish people. The wise men prepared gifts and took treasure chests with them on their journey to find the baby king.

Following the star
Matthew 2:2

The wise men traveled for many months until they reached Jerusalem. They stopped at the palace of King Herod and asked to see him. "We have come to see the baby who is born to be king of the Jews," they said. "We want to worship him."

The only king in Jerusalem

Matthew 2:3-8

King Herod was not happy. There was only room for one king in Jerusalem! He asked his priests where the prophecies said that a king would be born. Then he sent the wise men to Bethlehem. "Make sure you tell me when you find him. I may want to worship him, too…"

Wise men worship

Matthew 2:9-10

The wise men rode on their camels to Bethlehem, leaving King Herod behind. The star they had seen led them to a house in the village. When they entered the house they saw Mary with her little boy. They had found the baby king they were looking for.

Gifts for the baby king

Matthew 2:11

The wise men fell to their knees to worship Mary's little boy. Then they opened their treasure chests and offered the gifts they had brought with them. Mary's eyes opened wide as she saw gold, frankincense, and myrrh. Then the wise men left her. She thought about her strange and unexpected visitors and what their gifts could mean.

Wise men dream

Matthew 2:12

The wise men planned to return to their homes the next day, so they rested for the night. But God spoke to them in a dream. He warned them not to go back the way they had come. If they went back to Jerusalem, they would have to tell King Herod about Jesus. And King Herod had been plotting… So the wise men went back another way.

A home in Egypt
Matthew 2:13-23

Joseph also dreamed of angels that night. He woke Mary and told her that they must leave Bethlehem right away. King Herod was sending soldiers to find and destroy her child. Joseph, Mary, and Jesus made their home in Egypt until after Herod's death. Then they went to live in Nazareth in Galilee.

Celebrations in Jerusalem

Luke 2:41-42

When Jesus was twelve years old, Mary and Joseph took him to Jerusalem for the Passover festival as they did every year. Many people traveled together. It was a time of singing and praying to celebrate the time when Moses led the Israelites out of Egypt and from slavery to freedom.

Lost and found

Luke 2:43-52

On the way home, the group had been traveling for almost a whole day before Mary and Joseph realized that no one had seen Jesus. They returned to Jerusalem and anxiously looked for their son there. They found that he had been with the priests in the temple, who were amazed at all Jesus knew about God.

John the Baptist

Matthew 3:1-11

John, the son of Elizabeth and Zechariah, had grown into a man. He wore clothes made out of itchy camel's hair and ate the locusts and wild honey he could find in the desert. John was a prophet. He baptized people who turned away from the bad things they were doing and wanted to keep God's commandments. John was getting people ready for Jesus.

John baptizes Jesus
Matthew 3:13-17

Jesus was about the same age as John. One day he came to the River Jordan and asked John to baptize him. John knew that Jesus was God's Son. He knew that Jesus had done nothing bad, so he did not need to be forgiven. But when Jesus insisted, John baptized him anyway. Then everyone there heard God's voice. "This is my son. I love him."

Hard tests for Jesus

Matthew 4:1-7

After he was baptized, Jesus went into the desert to pray. During this time, Jesus had nothing to eat and he was very hungry. Then the devil came to test him. He asked Jesus to prove he was God's Son by turning stones into bread to eat and by throwing himself off the top of the temple. But Jesus would not give in when the devil tempted him.

The final temptation

Matthew 4:8-11

Then the devil took Jesus to a very high mountain. "Look at all this," the devil said. "I will give you everything if you will only worship me." Jesus was tired and hungry but he would not give in. "No! Leave me and go away," he said. "I will worship God, and God alone."

First followers

Luke 5:1-6

It was time for Jesus to start the work God had sent him to do. He found Peter and Andrew and asked them to take him out in their boat. "Throw out your nets and you'll have a good catch of fish," said Jesus. The men did as Jesus asked—and suddenly the nets were filled with fish!

Nets full of fish

Luke 5:7-11

There were so many silvery, wriggly fish that Peter and Andrew could not hold the net! They called to James and John, who came to help. "Follow me," Jesus said. The four fishermen decided to follow Jesus and were the first of twelve men who became his special friends, called disciples.

The wedding guests
John 2:1-4

Mary had been invited to a wedding in the village of Cana. She took Jesus and his friends along, too. It was a very happy day—until they ran out of wine. Mary was afraid that the bride and groom would be embarrassed in front of their guests. She did not want to spoil their happiness, so she asked Jesus to help them.

A miracle in Cana

John 2:5-11

"Fill those pots with water," Jesus asked the servants. They filled six huge water pots with cool water. "Take a cup from one of them to the man in charge of the feast." Jesus then said. The servants were amazed when they saw that the water had turned into the best wine. Jesus had performed a miracle.

213

The hole in the roof

Mark 2:1-4

Jesus was in Capernaum. So many people had come to listen to what he had to say that there was no space for any more visitors. But four men needed Jesus to help their friend. The poor man could not walk. The four men climbed up the steps outside the house—and made a hole in the roof! Then they lowered their friend through the hole.

A miracle in Capernaum
Mark 2:5-12

The people below helped the man to the floor. "It's okay," Jesus said. "You can get up and carry your mat home now. I have healed you." The man did as Jesus asked—and everyone was amazed! Jesus was saying and doing things that only God could do. But not everyone thought this was a good thing. The religious leaders did not like it at all.

Matthew, the tax collector

Matthew 9:9-13

Matthew was busy. He collected taxes for the Romans. "Come and follow me, Matthew!" Jesus called to him—and Matthew left his booth and followed Jesus. People went up to Jesus' friends and asked them what Jesus was doing. Surely Jesus should have nothing to do with bad people like the tax collectors? "These people need me," said Jesus. "That's why I am here."

Happy people
Matthew 5:1-12

Jesus sat down on a hillside and people gathered to listen to him. "God blesses people who are not too proud to ask for his help. God comforts people who are sad and God will be kind to people who are kind to others. Long for things that are good—and God will satisfy you."

Be different!

Matthew 5:43-44

"Don't be afraid to be different. Loving God means being perfect, like Him. Love people and treat them kindly—even if they are not kind to you. Forgive them if they hurt you. Treat them as you would like to be treated," said Jesus. "Love your enemies and pray for them."

Take time to pray
Matthew 6:5-8

"Find a place to be alone. Talk to God as if you are talking to a father who loves you," said Jesus. "Be honest and tell God what you feel. Share with Him what worries you. God doesn't need special words—and He knows what you need already. God cares about you. He will help you."

Pray to the Lord

Matthew 6:9-13

"God wants us to talk to Him like a father who loves his child. Say something like, "Father, You are great and holy. Please make the place where we live full of peace and kindness and justice, just like heaven. Give us what we need to eat today and forgive us if we have hurt other people, just as we will forgive people who have hurt us."

God cares about you

Matthew 6:25-34

"Don't worry about the things you need every day," said Jesus. "God feeds the birds and He makes the flowers beautiful. They don't need to worry. God cares even more about you than He cares about the birds above you or the flowers around you. You can trust God to give you everything you need."

The soldier in Capernaum
Matthew 8:5-7

There was a Roman soldier in Capernaum who had made friends among the people there. He had even built a synagogue for them. The soldier knew all about Jesus. So when his servant became ill, he asked Jesus to help him.

Jesus heals the soldier's servant

Matthew 8:8-13

"You don't need to come to my house," the soldier said. "I know you can heal him. Just say that he is healed and I know that he will be." Jesus was amazed at the soldier's faith. "God welcomes everyone everywhere to trust Him, and you are right to trust me now. Your servant is well again." And he was.

Very frightened friends
Luke 8:22-23

It was a calm evening when Jesus got into the boat to sail across Lake Galilee with his friends. Jesus was very tired and soon fell asleep. But, as sometimes happened, a wind came from nowhere and the weather changed suddenly. The little boat lurched up and down on choppy waves. "Jesus! Wake up! Help us!" his friends called out. Jesus stood up and took control.

Jesus calms the storm

Luke 8:24-25

"Peace!" Jesus spoke to the howling wind. "Be still!" Jesus called to the choppy waves. Within seconds the wind dropped and the waves became gentle ripples on the surface of the water. The frightened men felt the soft breeze on their faces once more. "Why were you so afraid?" Jesus asked them. "Didn't you know I would look after you?"

Nicodemus' secret visit

John 3:1-17

Not many of the religious leaders liked Jesus. But Nicodemus wanted to understand more about what Jesus taught about God. One night, he went to see Jesus. "God sent me here to save people," Jesus told him. "God loves the world so much that He has given his only Son so that anyone who believes in me can live forever."

The woman at the well

John 4:4-26

A woman was drawing water from a well in Samaria. "Can I have some water?" Jesus asked her. "Why ask me—you Jews don't usually talk to Samaritans," she replied. "I know everything about you," said Jesus. "I can offer you water that will stop you ever being thirsty again. I am the one you are waiting for, sent by God to save you."

The woman who needed help

Luke 8:43-48

Jesus was on his way to help Jairus' little daughter. As he walked through the crowd, he stopped suddenly. "Who touched me?" he asked. The disciples could see that everyone was touching him—there were hundreds of people there. But a woman spoke shyly to Jesus. "I only touched the hem of your robe," she said. "I knew you could make me well." Jesus smiled at her as he turned to move on.

The little girl who needed help
Luke 8:49-56

Someone was coming toward them through the crowd. "Don't hurry," they shouted. "It's too late, she's dead." Jairus looked at Jesus. This was terrible—his daughter was only twelve. "Trust me," said Jesus. He went into the house and knelt beside the body. "Get up, little girl," he said. And she sat up, feeling much better.

A little boy's lunch
Luke 9:12-16

Thousands of people had come to hear Jesus; some also needed to be healed. Now it was late. "Can we find food for them all?" Jesus asked his disciples. "There's a boy offering his lunch—but it's only five pieces of bread and two dried fishes," said Andrew. "Thank you," Jesus said to the boy. Then he thanked God for the food, too.

Lots of leftovers
Luke 9:16-17

Jesus shared the food with the disciples and asked them to share it with the people in the crowd. Everyone enjoyed the food; they had plenty to eat so that at the end, the disciples collected up twelve baskets with leftovers. It was a miracle. Jesus had given food to over 5,000 people—by sharing a boy's packed lunch.

Jesus heals a deaf man
Mark 7:32-37

Jesus could hear the birds calling over the sea and the wind in the trees; but the man standing in front of him could hear nothing at all. His friends stood some distance away, waiting. Could Jesus help a deaf man to hear? Jesus touched the man's ears and his tongue. Then suddenly everyone was smiling! The man ran to his friends!

The story of the good Samaritan
Luke 10:30-37

"A man was attacked on the road from Jerusalem to Jericho." Jesus was telling one of his stories. "A priest and a Levite walked right past him. But a Samaritan stopped and bandaged the man's wounds. He paid for him to be looked after until he was well. If you want to know what it means to love other people," said Jesus, "be like the good Samaritan."

The story of the lost sheep
Luke 15:3-7

"If you have a hundred sheep but find that one has gone missing—what do you do?" Jesus asked. "You search until you find your lost sheep. Then you carry him home on your shoulders. God is like that. He cares about everyone, especially the one that is lonely and lost."

The story of the loving father

Luke 15:11-32

"One day a young man left his father's home," said Jesus. "When all his money was gone, he took a job feeding smelly pigs. He hated it! Finally he went home to say he was sorry. But his father had been waiting for him. He was so happy he threw a party! God is like that. He loves his children and waits for them to come to Him."

The story of the very rich man

Luke 12:16-20

"Once there was a very rich farmer," said Jesus. "One year he had a very good harvest. So he pulled down his barns and built bigger ones where he could store all his crops. He planned to relax and enjoy his money and all the good things he had stored up for himself. But that night, the man died."

Treasure in heaven

Luke 12:21, 33-34

"What good were his riches to him now?" said Jesus. "Don't be greedy. Life is more important than the things money can buy. Share what you have with people who need it. Then you will store up treasure in heaven where moths cannot eat it and robbers cannot break in and steal it."

Waiting for Jesus
Luke 17:11-13

Ten men stood at the edge of a village. Their clothes were ragged and they were covered in bandages. They were waiting for Jesus. The men had leprosy, a nasty skin disease. This meant they had to live away from their families so they wouldn't make them ill, too.
"Help us, Jesus!" they cried.

Only one said "Thank you!"

Luke 17:14-18

Most people were afraid to go near the lepers. But Jesus welcomed them. "I have made you well," he said. The men could not wait to go home to their families! One man stopped to kneel at Jesus' feet. "Thank you, Lord, for healing me!" he said. Jesus smiled. "But where are the other nine men? Why didn't they return to give praise to God?" he asked sadly.

Mary, Martha, and Lazarus
John 11: 1-7

Lazarus lived in Bethany with his two sisters. Jesus often went to stay with them. They were good friends. Jesus was traveling one day when someone brought him a message—Lazarus was very ill. Martha and Mary wanted Jesus to come quickly and make their brother well, but it was a few days before Jesus arrived in Bethany.

Jesus comforts Martha

John 11:17-22

Martha was waiting for Jesus. She had very sad news. "My brother died," she told him. "We buried him four days ago. If only you had been here, I know Lazarus would still be alive." Jesus comforted her. "Your brother will live again," he told her. "I have power over life and death. Anyone who trusts me will never die." Martha nodded. "I know you are God's Son," she said.

Lazarus lives again!

John 11:34-44

Many people had come to comfort the sisters. They came now with Mary to show Jesus where Lazarus had been buried. Jesus was so sad that he cried with them—even though he knew what would happen next. "Father God," Jesus prayed, "let all these people know that You have sent me to help them." Then Jesus called to Lazarus to come out of the tomb. Everyone was amazed when Lazarus walked out. He was alive!

Jesus welcomes children

Mark 10:13-16

Wherever Jesus went, mothers brought their children so he could bless them. Children liked to be where Jesus was. But sometimes the disciples tried to keep them away. They thought Jesus was too busy or too tired. "My kingdom is made up of people like these children," Jesus said. "They are ready to love and trust God with all their hearts. Don't ever stop them from coming to me. They are always welcome."

Blind Bartimaeus

Mark 10:46-47

Jesus had been visiting Jericho. His disciples were following him. Many people had gathered to listen to Jesus and were also following him. The crowd made quite a noise. So although blind Bartimaeus could not see Jesus, as he sat begging by the roadside, he soon found out that he was nearby. "Jesus, please help me!" he shouted.

The blind man sees!

Mark 10:48-52

"Jesus is too busy!" people said. But Bartimaeus would not be put off. He called out again. Jesus stopped. He asked his disciples to call the beggar over. Bartimaeus stumbled over to Jesus. "Please help me to see!" the blind man said. "Because you trust me, you will be healed," Jesus said. "Go now; you can see."

The little tax collector

Luke 19:1-4

What was Zacchaeus, the tax collector, doing up a tree? He wanted to see Jesus—and no one would let him through the crowd that had gathered. Everyone knew Zacchaeus was a cheat. But Jesus knew he was there. He stopped and looked up at the man clinging to the branches.

Zacchaeus meets Jesus

Luke 19:5-10

"Come down, Zacchaeus!" Jesus said. "I'd like to come to your house today." The people in the crowd frowned. Why would Jesus be nice to a man who stole from them? But Jesus knew that Zacchaeus needed him. "That's why I'm here," Jesus said later. "I want to help people see that doing bad things doesn't make them happy." Everything changed for Zacchaeus that day. He became an honest man.

Living God's way

Matthew 25:31-40

"God sees how we live," Jesus told his disciples. "He will be pleased with those who have been kind—those who gave food to the hungry, or shared what they have with others; those who visited people in prison or in the hospital. If you are kind to anyone else, it's the same as if you are kind to me."

Living selfishly
Matthew 25:41-46

"God is sad when He sees people turn their backs on those who are cold or hungry, in prison or in the hospital," said Jesus. "God is sad when people live only to please themselves. God cares about everyone, and he wants us to live the same way."

A feast in Bethany

John 12:1-8

Lazarus had arranged a special dinner for Jesus in Bethany. Martha served a feast for him while Lazarus sat at the table. Then Mary came and poured expensive perfume over Jesus' feet, drying them with her long hair. "We could have sold that," Judas said crossly, "but now she has wasted it." Jesus shook his head. "Mary has done something out of love and kindness," he answered. "She has anointed me ready for my death."

The King comes to Jerusalem

Luke 19:29-39

Jesus rode on a donkey toward the city of Jerusalem. He and his friends had come for the Passover feast. Crowds lined the roads and spread their cloaks in front of Jesus. They waved huge palm branches. "Praise God!" they cheered. "Here comes Jesus, our King!" But some of the religious leaders were also in the crowd. "Stop that shouting," they said angrily.

Chaos in the temple

Matthew 21:12-15

Jesus went to the temple to pray, but he was angry at what he saw there. There was not peace but chaos. People were selling animals for offerings. Money-changers were arguing with visitors. "Stop!" Jesus shouted as he turned over their tables. "You are making God's house into a marketplace!" Then Jesus turned to the people who needed his help, some blind, some unable to walk, and he healed them.

The woman who gave everything
Mark 12:41-44

Rich people were putting money into the collection box in the temple. But Jesus was more interested in a poor widow. "This woman really loves God," Jesus said to his friends. "The others are giving lots of money but, they have plenty left over to spend on themselves. She has given God everything that she has."

Plots and plans
Matthew 26:1-4

"In two days' time, we will celebrate the Passover feast," Jesus told his friends. "But this is also the time when they will come to arrest me and take me away to be crucified." Meanwhile the priests and religious leaders were plotting. "We must stop Jesus from talking to the people," they agreed. "But we must be careful—everyone loves him. We don't want a riot."

Be kind to each other

John 13:4-20

Peter was not happy. The disciples were all together in an upstairs room and Jesus was preparing to wash their feet. "No!" said Peter. "This is the job of a servant." But Jesus insisted gently. "That is why I am doing this, Peter," he said. "None of us is better than the rest. You need to show that you care about each other so people know that you follow me."

Friends around the table

John 13:21-26

Jesus looked around the table as they sat down to eat supper. "You are my friends," he said. "But soon one of you will betray me to my enemies." John was sitting beside Jesus. "But who would do this?" he asked. Judas looked away from Jesus and fidgeted on his seat. Jesus dipped some bread in oil and gave it to him. Then to John, Jesus said, "The one who took the bread."

Eleven friends left

John 13:27-30

Then Jesus spoke to Judas. "Go now, and do what you have to do." Judas took one last look at the group around the table. Then he left the room and went out into the night. Judas was the group's treasurer. The others thought that he was going to give money to the poor. Money was jingling in his pocket—the thirty silver coins he had been given to lead armed men to Jesus.

Peter's brave words

John 13:31-38

"It is almost time for me to leave you," Jesus told his friends. "Love each other in the way that I have loved you and taken care of you." "But where are you going?" asked Peter. "I would do anything for you!" Jesus looked sad. "I know, Peter. Yet before the rooster crows tomorrow morning, you will have said three times that you do not even know me."

Bread and wine

Mark 14:22-25

Jesus and his friends ate their last supper together. Jesus broke the bread and shared it with them. "Eat this," he said. "This is my body which will be broken for you." Then Jesus took a cup of wine and said, "Drink this. This is my blood which will be shed for you."

Jesus prays
Matthew 26:36-38

Jesus led his friends to a garden called Gethsemane where he liked to pray in the quiet of the olive trees. "Please stay here and keep watch," Jesus asked Peter, John, and James. "Pray for me." Jesus went on a little farther so he could talk to God by himself.

Jesus is alone

Matthew 26:39

Jesus knew that soon people would come to arrest him. Soon he would be taken away from his friends. Soon he would be very much alone. "Please help me, Father," he asked God. "Help me to be brave. I wish You could take away all the suffering that is soon to happen. But if I must die tomorrow, help me not to be afraid."

Sleeping friends
Matthew 26:40-46

When Jesus went back to see his friends, they were not keeping watch. They were not even praying for him. All the disciples—even Peter, John, and James—had fallen asleep. Jesus woke them. "Could you not pray for just a little while?" he asked them. Jesus went away to pray again—but his friends just couldn't stay awake.

Judas leads armed guards

Matthew 26:47-56

There were lights in the garden. There was the sound of men walking through the trees. "It is time," said Jesus. The disciples recognized Judas leading a band of armed men. They stared when he stepped forward to kiss Jesus as if he was his friend. Judas had betrayed Jesus to his enemies.

Jesus, the prisoner
Mark 14:46-50

Men surrounded Jesus and made him their prisoner. His friends were so afraid, they ran away and left him. Then the men with swords and clubs marched Jesus away though the trees and into the night. Peter waited until they were well ahead of him. Then he followed, keeping out of sight.

Peter weeps
Luke 22:54-62

Peter waited outside while Jesus was inside the high priest's house. "This man is one of his friends," said a girl who had been watching him. "No, I'm not!" said Peter quickly. "Yes," said another, "I think you're right." Peter denied it again. "He even has the same accent as Jesus," a man said later. "It's not true!" Peter said. "I told you—I don't know Jesus!" Then the rooster crowed. Peter wept as he remembered what Jesus had said.

The angry crowd
Matthew 27:11-22

Pontius Pilate, the Roman governor, was the next person to question Jesus. Only he could decide if someone should die. Pilate could tell Jesus was innocent, but he knew the priests wanted him dead. Outside, a bloodthirsty crowd was shouting, "Crucify him! Crucify him!"

The crown of thorns

Matthew 27:22-31

"It is almost Passover," Pilate said to the crowd. "I can release a prisoner. Do you want Barabbas, the murderer? Or this man, Jesus from Nazareth?" The shout went up: "Set Barabbas free! Crucify Jesus!" Pilate gave Jesus to the soldiers. They dressed him in a scarlet robe, pushed a crown of thorns onto his head, and made fun of the man they called "King Jesus."

On Friday morning
John 19:17

Jesus stumbled as the soldiers marched him away to be crucified outside the city walls. Some of the people watching him had been his friends. They had heard Jesus talk about love and kindness. They had seen him heal people they knew. They knew he was a good man and they wept for him.

A cross between two thieves

Luke 23:32-38

Jesus was made to carry the piece of wood on which he would be crucified. When he reached the place, the soldiers put a sign above him saying: "This is the King of the Jews." Then they nailed him there, between two thieves. "Forgive them," Jesus prayed to God. "They don't know what they are doing."

Crosses on the hillside

Luke 23:39-43

As they were dying, one of the thieves spoke to Jesus from his cross. "You saved other people—why don't you save yourself?" But the other thief answered him. "Leave him alone! We deserve to be punished, but this man has done nothing wrong. Jesus, please remember me." Jesus promised that he would be with the thief that day in heaven.

John and Mary

John 19:26-27

Among the others who were there while Jesus was on the cross were his mother Mary and friend John. "Mother!" Jesus cried out. "This is your son now. John! Take care of Mary for me." Mary was weeping and John comforted her. Hours passed and Jesus became weaker.

The Son of God

Matthew 27:46-51,54

Jesus knew that he was dying for others and not for himself. He knew that this was why he had been born. But now he felt very much alone. Jesus cried out in a loud voice and then he died. At that moment the earth shook. The soldier near his cross said, "This man really was the Son of God."

The death of Jesus

Matthew 27:55-58

Some of the women among Jesus' friends stood weeping by the cross. It was almost the start of the Sabbath, and they did not want his body left there. Joseph from Arimathea went to Pilate and asked if he could bury Jesus in his own tomb. Pilate agreed. The soldiers put a sword in Jesus' side to make sure that he was dead.

Friends bury Jesus

John 19:38-42

Joseph went with Nicodemus and took Jesus' body down from the cross. They carried him to the garden, where a new tomb had been carved in the rock, and wrapped his body in spices and a clean linen sheet. The men closed the tomb tightly by rolling a large stone across the entrance.

Mary Magdalene weeps
Matthew 27:61, Luke 8:2

That Friday evening the women followed Joseph and Nicodemus. They wanted to see where the men laid Jesus so they could come after the Sabbath to anoint his body properly. Jesus had been kind to Mary Magdalene. Others had made her an outcast. Jesus had healed her and been her friend. She wept for him.

Early Sunday morning

Luke 23:55—24:1

The Sabbath had started at dusk on Friday evening. The women, along with all Jesus' friends, had rested on Saturday. They had spent time praying and worshiping God. But it was not the same without Jesus there. Now that the Sabbath was over, Mary Magdalene left her house before the sun was up.

The garden tomb
Luke 24:1

Mary went to collect Joanna and Mary, the mother of James, and together they went to the garden where they had seen Joseph and Nicodemus lay Jesus' body in a new tomb. They took with them the spices they had prepared to anoint his body.

Who moved the stone?

Mark 16:2-4

So it was that very early on Sunday morning, the women came into the garden. They had been wondering how they would be able to roll away the stone door that closed the tomb. But when they arrived, the stone had already been rolled away! The tomb was empty!

The message of the angels
Luke 24:3-8

Just as they were puzzling over what could have happened, and why the body of Jesus was not there, two angels appeared. "Why are you looking for Jesus here among the dead? Don't you remember— he told you he would rise from the dead on the third day. He is alive!"

The empty tomb
Luke 24:9-11

Then the women could not wait to tell Jesus' other friends what they had seen. They ran back to the city and told the eleven disciples and then anyone else who knew Jesus that the stone had been rolled away and Jesus was not there! The men could not believe the news. They had to see for themselves.

John believes

John 20:3-8

So Peter and John ran from the city to the garden. They saw that the body of Jesus had gone—just as the women had said. The linen that had wrapped his body was lying on the shelf, empty. Then John realized what had happened—and believed that Jesus had risen from the dead—and that he was alive!

Mary meets Jesus

John 20:10-17

The men returned to the city, leaving Mary alone in the garden. Her eyes were clouded with tears when she heard a voice behind her saying her name. She knew that voice—it was Jesus! She was delighted to see him alive and able to speak to her! "Go and tell the others that you have seen me," said Jesus.

The good news of Jesus

John 20:18

Mary ran back again to see the eleven disciples. This time she was not confused—she was very happy. She gave them the good news. "I have seen him!" she told them as soon as she caught her breath. "Jesus really is alive—and I have seen him!"

Inside a locked room

John 20:19-29

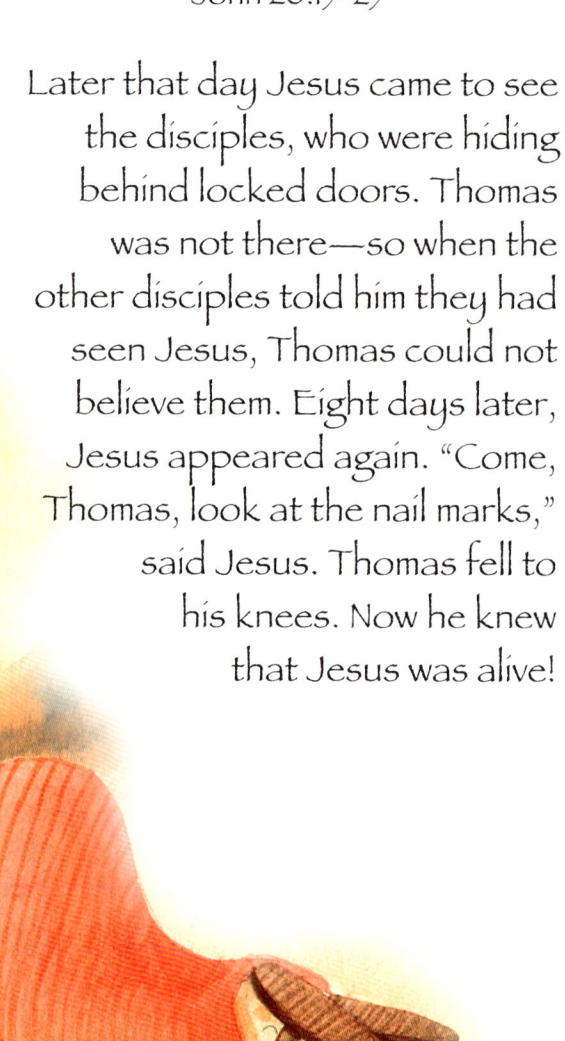

Later that day Jesus came to see the disciples, who were hiding behind locked doors. Thomas was not there—so when the other disciples told him they had seen Jesus, Thomas could not believe them. Eight days later, Jesus appeared again. "Come, Thomas, look at the nail marks," said Jesus. Thomas fell to his knees. Now he knew that Jesus was alive!

Sunrise on Lake Galilee

John 21:4-6

Jesus stood on the shore beside Lake Galilee at sunrise. He was warming bread over a little fire—and could see some of his friends in their fishing boat. "Throw your net on the right side of the boat!" he called.

The huge catch of fish

John 21:1-3, 6

Peter, James, John, Thomas, and a few others had been fishing all night. Now the sun was rising and they had still caught nothing. But they put their net on the other side of the boat as the man on the shore suggested. A few minutes later, their net was bursting with fish and they were hauling in the catch!

Peter is forgiven
John 21:7-17

Peter suddenly realized that the man was Jesus! A short while later they were all eating bread and fish together. Peter was quiet. He still felt guilty that he had denied Jesus the night that he was arrested. "Do you love me, Peter?" Jesus asked. "Yes, Lord, you know I do!" Peter replied. Then Jesus gave Peter the job of taking care of all his friends.

Jesus returns to his Father

Acts 1:1-11

Jesus met his disciples many more times until it was time for him to return to be with God in heaven. "I will come back one day," he told them. "But wait now for the Holy Spirit to give you power to do great things." Jesus then left his friends and returned to heaven.

Power at Pentecost

Acts 2:1-4

People had come from all over the world to celebrate the feast of Pentecost in Jerusalem. Jesus' friends were all together when a sound like a rushing wind filled their house. The Holy Spirit had come to give them strength to do the good things that Jesus wanted them to do.

Peter talks about Jesus

Acts 2:14-41

Now Peter was no longer the fisherman he had been. The Holy Spirit helped him to talk about Jesus to the crowd that had gathered. "Jesus died on a cross—but God has given him new life! Believe that Jesus is the Son of God and he will forgive the bad things you have done." About 3,000 people became Christians that day.

More than silver or gold

Acts 3:1-10

Soon afterwards Peter and John went to the temple to pray. A man there who couldn't walk begged them for money. "I have no silver or gold to give you," said Peter, "but I can heal you in Jesus' name—which is much better!" Then the man was able to get up and walk—and he thanked God for healing him.

Inside a prison cell

Acts 4:1-3

People were amazed to see the lame man walk again. But not everyone was happy about it. The temple guards had thought that the death of Jesus would be the end of their problems—but it seemed to be just the beginning. They arrested Peter and John and put them in prison.

Peter speaks out
Acts 4:7-20

Peter answered bravely when he was asked what had happened. "Jesus healed the man—you have seen the miracle for yourselves." The temple guards did not dare keep Peter and John in prison for long because so many people were praising God for the miracle. The guards told the prisoners that they must not speak about Jesus again. "But it's such good news—how can we keep it to ourselves?" Peter replied.

Stephen is arrested

Acts 4:4, 32-35; 6:1—7:57

There were now about 5,000 people in Jerusalem, living the way that Jesus had taught them, sharing everything they owned. God blessed Stephen so that he healed people who were ill and spoke bravely about Jesus. The temple elders arrested Stephen and arranged for him to be stoned to death.

The death of Stephen

Acts 7:58—8:1; 9:1-2

Saul stood by and watched as Stephen died. He was pleased. Saul believed in God—but he was sure that the followers of Jesus were wrong. He made it his aim to find them all and put them in prison.

On the road to Gaza

Acts 8:26-30

Life was not easy for the people who followed Jesus—but they knew that they had his help. Some left Jerusalem but wherever they went, they told people about Jesus. Philip offered to help a man from Ethiopia on the road to Gaza. The man was sitting in a chariot, reading about Jesus.

A new believer

Acts 8:31-38

"Can you help me?" the man asked Philip. "I don't understand this prophecy." So Philip explained all he knew about Jesus—that he had died on a cross so that anyone who trusted him could be forgiven. The man wanted to be baptized right away, so Philip baptized him.

Saul travels to Damascus

Acts 9:1-4

Saul went with some friends to Damascus to look for more Christians. He wanted to put them all in prison. But on the way, something happened that changed his life forever. Saul saw a bright light from heaven that blinded him and he heard the voice of Jesus. "Saul, why are you hurting me? Why are you hurting my friends?"

Saul's mission

Acts 9:6-19

Saul's friends had heard the voice of Jesus, too. Now they had to lead Saul to Damascus because he could not see. Saul spent the next three days praying. God told him that a man named Ananias would come to heal him of his blindness. "Saul will help people all over the world to understand who Jesus is," God told Ananias. So Saul was healed and baptized a Christian.

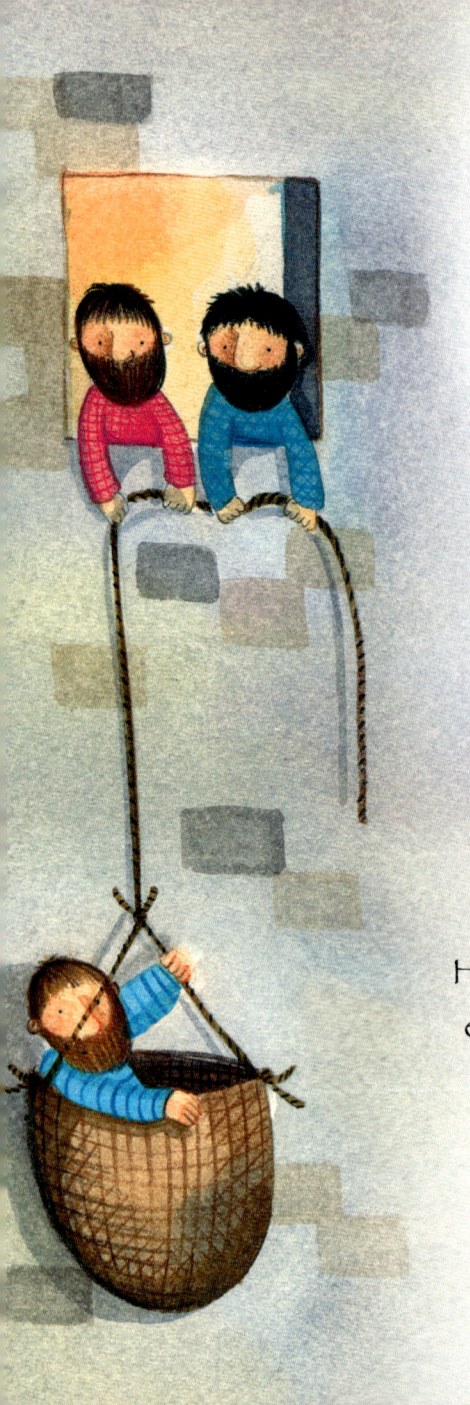

Saul becomes Paul

Acts 9:20-25

Saul now became known as Paul. And he couldn't wait to tell everyone about Jesus. No one could believe the change in him. But this meant that he made enemies. The people who had encouraged him to find Christians and put them in prison now came after him! His new friends had to help him escape secretly from a window in the city walls.

Cornelius meets an angel

Acts 10:1-7

Cornelius was a soldier in the Roman army. But he loved God, prayed often, and gave generously to the poor. He was surprised one day by an angel who told him to find Peter, who was staying in Joppa by the sea. Peter would help him understand all he wanted to know. So Cornelius sent men to Joppa to find Peter.

Peter's strange vision

Acts 10:9-48

Meanwhile, Peter also had a vision. He saw a sheet full of animals which he was told to eat. "But these animals are forbidden to your people," he told God. "Not anymore," God answered. Peter understood that everyone was now welcome in God's kingdom. When Peter met Cornelius later, he baptized the soldier and his family.

Peter in chains

Acts 12:1-6

The new king in Judea had James, one of the first disciples, executed. Then Peter was put in chains in prison awaiting his own death, with a guard on either side of him and soldiers guarding the door. Everyone was afraid. Peter's friends met together to pray for his safety.

A miracle in the prison

Acts 12:7-17

God answered their prayers. He sent an angel to Peter's prison cell, where the chains fell off his wrists and the doors and gates opened by themselves! Peter followed the angel past the guards and outside to freedom. Then he went to his friends' house to tell them of the miracle he had seen. They could hardly believe it!

Paul in trouble

Acts 14:8-19

Paul traveled from place to place. Sometimes he was welcomed. In Lystra he and Barnabas healed a man who couldn't walk—but when people saw this, they tried to worship them. "No—we are not gods—we worship the one true God who made heaven and earth and gives us power to heal," Paul told them. But the crowd would not listen. Later they became angry and stoned Paul, leaving him badly injured.

Earthquakes and miracles

Acts 16:22-34

In Philippi, Paul and his friend Silas were beaten and put in prison with their feet in the stocks. Around midnight when they were singing hymns and praying, there was an earthquake and their chains fell off. The prison guard drew his sword to kill himself, thinking his prisoners would escape. Paul stopped him. "But how can I be saved?" the guard asked. "Trust Jesus and be baptized!" Paul answered. So that day the guard and all his family became Christians.

Paul's journeys
Acts 13—20

When Paul and Silas were released from prison, they continued their work. They shared with people everywhere the news that Jesus had died on a cross so that they could be forgiven. People listened and were baptized. They started new Christian churches in many different places.

Paul's sufferings

Acts 23:1—27:41

Paul had often been attacked, beaten, and imprisoned. He didn't care as long as people knew about Jesus. But after years in prison, he asked to stand trial under the emperor because he was a Roman citizen. Luke traveled with Paul on the ship heading for Rome. The boat was caught in a violent storm, and Luke and Paul were shipwrecked with all the other prisoners.

Safe at last

Acts 27:42—28:10

Paul knew that God would not let them die. All 276 people on board reached land by clinging to parts of the broken ship. The people on the island of Malta then took care of them until it was safe to get another boat to Rome. During the months they were there, Paul healed people who were ill and told them about Jesus, too.

Living in Rome
Acts 28:11-31

When Paul arrived in Rome, he was allowed to live under house arrest. People could visit him and Paul could tell them about Jesus—but there was always a soldier there to guard him.

Paul wrote letters to Christians in all the places he had visited, encouraging them to follow Jesus and helping them with the problems they had as new Christians.
"The most important thing you can do," wrote Paul, "is to love other people. Don't gossip or tell lies. Don't be proud or rude. Don't be greedy or remind people of the bad things they have done. Put other people before yourself. Look after them. That's the best way to show them that you love God."

The Old Testament

In the beginning 6
God makes plants and trees 7
God makes the sun, moon, and stars 8
God makes fish and sea creatures 9
God makes birds and butterflies 10
God makes all the animals 11
God makes people 12
God rests 13
The garden of Eden 14
The sneaky serpent 15
Everything is spoiled 16
Adam and Eve's children 17
Cain and Abel 18
Cain kills his brother 19

God's plan 20
Noah builds an ark 21
Two by two 22
The flood 23
The raven and the dove 24
Leaving the ark 25
The rainbow 26
God speaks to Abraham 27
A home in Canaan 28
God blesses Abraham 29
Three special visitors 30
Little baby Isaac 31
A sad day for Abraham 32
The very special gift 33
God's blessing 34
A special wife for Isaac 35

The answer to a prayer 36
Two little boys 37
Esau and Jacob 38
Esau's silly promise 39
A father's blessing 40
A mother's wish 41
Jacob tricks his father 42
Jacob is sent away 43
Jacob's ladder 44
Jacob falls in love 45
Laban's unkind trick 46
Everyone is happy! 47
Lots of wives and children! 48
Time to go home 49
Jacob tricks his uncle 50
Friends and brothers 51

Jacob's favorite son 52	Jacob's blessing........................ 68	The final plague......................... 83
Joseph, the dreamer 53	Joseph dies in Egypt................ 69	The Passover 84
The plot begins......................... 54	Slaves in Egypt 70	The king says, "Go!" 85
Things go wrong for Joseph...... 55	The baby in the basket................71	God leads his people 86
The long walk to Egypt 56	Moses and the princess............. 72	Crossing the Red Sea 87
Sold as a slave to Potiphar 57	Moses runs away 73	Learning to trust God............... 88
Things go wrong again 58	From prince to shepherd 74	Food in the desert 89
Dreams and more dreams 59	The burning bush 75	Mountaintop experience 90
Two years later......................... 60	"Let my people go!" 76	The Ten Commandments 91
God's warning 61	The first plague 77	Down the mountain................... 92
Good harvests and bad............. 62	The plague of frogs................... 78	The golden calf........................... 93
Famine in Israel.......................... 63	The plagues of gnats and flies 79	Moses prays for God's people........................... 94
Ten men from Canaan 64	A terrible time in Egypt.............80	Priests and helpers 95
Sacks of grain.............................. 65	The plague of hailstones 81	A special agreement 96
Joseph's silver cup..................... 66	The eighth and ninth plagues 82	Twelve spies 97
Joseph weeps for joy 67		

The Old Testament

The spies' report 98	Naomi's sadness 114	Goliath the champion 130
Joshua, the new leader 99	Ruth's kindness 115	Bears and lions 131
Spies in Jericho! 100	Ruth meets Boaz 116	David fights the giant 132
A narrow escape 101	Naomi's little grandson 117	David and Jonathan 133
The fast-flowing river 102	Hannah's prayer 118	King David 134
A safe crossing 103	God calls Samuel 119	David's big temptation 135
The city of Jericho 104	Samuel, prophet and judge 120	David's big mistake 136
Walls come tumbling down 105	Israel wants a king 121	The prophet, Nathan 137
The land of Canaan 106	Wandering donkeys 122	David weeps 138
Broken promises 107	The first king of Israel 123	God blesses David 139
A prophet called Deborah 108	The people's king 124	David's son, Absalom 140
A brave woman's victory 109	Things go wrong 125	Solomon's dream 141
God chooses Gideon 110	Seven handsome sons 126	Wise King Solomon 142
A sign for Gideon 111	The eighth son of Jesse 127	Solomon's temple 143
A very small army 112	Music for King Saul 128	God's house 144
A victory for God 113	The shepherd's song 129	The queen of Sheba 145

A bad king and a wicked queen 146	God forgives 161	The writing on the wall 177
No more rain 147	God's plans for Jeremiah 162	God tests Belshazzar 178
God takes care of Elijah 148	The potter and the clay............163	Daniel, the governor 179
The oil that never ran out 149	A warning for the king 164	Plots against Daniel..................180
Time to choose 150	Babylon—the enemy.................165	In the lions' den 181
The prophets of Baal 151	Alone in a dark well...................166	Nehemiah wants to go home 182
Elijah's prayer 152	A friend for Jeremiah................167	An answer to prayer 183
Fire and rain..............................153	Jerusalem is destroyed.............168	Home at last 184
Jezebel's threats......................154	Jeremiah stays in Jerusalem 169	God's promised Savior...............185
Chariot of fire...........................155	The strange land of Babylon....170	
The little servant girl 156	A very hard task 171	
God heals Naaman....................157	God helps Daniel 172	
Jonah is sent to Nineveh...........158	The king's strange dream..........173	
Jonah hides from God 159	Daniel's three friends................174	
Swallowed by a big fish 160	The fiery furnace......................175	
	King Belshazzar of Babylon 176	

The New Testament

An angel in the temple 188	First followers 210	A little boy's lunch 230
Good news for Elizabeth 189	Nets full of fish 211	Lots of leftovers 231
Mary's special secret 190	The wedding guests 212	Jesus heals a deaf man 232
Mary and Elizabeth 191	A miracle in Cana 213	The story of the good Samaritan 233
The Roman census 192	The hole in the roof 214	The story of the lost sheep 234
No room at the inn 193	A miracle in Capernaum 215	The story of the loving father 235
Shepherds on the hillside 194	Matthew, the tax collector 216	The story of the very rich man 236
Angels in the sky 195	Happy people 217	Treasure in heaven 237
The baby in the manger 196	Be different! 218	Waiting for Jesus 238
Wise men in the East 197	Take time to pray 219	Only one said "Thank you!" 239
Following the star 198	Pray to the Lord 220	Mary, Martha, and Lazarus 240
The only king in Jerusalem 199	God cares about you 221	Jesus comforts Martha 241
Wise men worship 200	The soldier in Capernaum 222	Lazarus lives again! 242
Gifts for the baby king 201	Jesus heals the soldier's servant 223	Jesus welcomes children 243
Wise men dream 202	Very frightened friends 224	Blind Bartimaeus 244
A home in Egypt 203	Jesus calms the storm 225	The blind man sees! 245
Celebrations in Jerusalem 204	Nicodemus' secret visit 226	The little tax collector 246
Lost and found 205	The woman at the well 227	Zacchaeus meets Jesus 247
John the Baptist 206	The woman who needed help 228	Living God's way 248
John baptizes Jesus 207	The little girl who needed help 229	Living selfishly 249
Hard tests for Jesus 208		
The final temptation 209		

A feast in Bethany 250	Crosses on the hillside 270	More than silver or gold 291
The King comes to Jerusalem 251	John and Mary 271	Inside a prison cell 292
Chaos in the temple 252	The Son of God 272	Peter speaks out 293
The woman who gave everything 253	The death of Jesus 273	Stephen is arrested 294
Plots and plans 254	Friends bury Jesus 274	The death of Stephen 295
Be kind to each other 255	Mary Magdalene weeps 275	On the road to Gaza 296
Friends around the table 256	Early Sunday morning 276	A new believer 297
Eleven friends left 257	The garden tomb 277	Saul travels to Damascus 298
Peter's brave words 258	Who moved the stone? 278	Saul's mission 299
Bread and wine 259	The message of the angels 279	Saul becomes Paul 300
Jesus prays 260	The empty tomb 280	Cornelius meets an angel 301
Jesus is alone 261	John believes 281	Peter's strange vision 302
Sleeping friends 262	Mary meets Jesus 282	Peter in chains 303
Judas leads armed guards 263	The good news of Jesus 283	A miracle in the prison 304
Jesus, the prisoner 264	Inside a locked room 284	Paul in trouble 305
Peter weeps 265	Sunrise on Lake Galilee 285	Earthquakes and miracles 306
The angry crowd 266	The huge catch of fish 286	Paul's journeys 307
The crown of thorns 267	Peter is forgiven 287	Paul's sufferings 308
On Friday morning 268	Jesus returns to his Father 288	Safe at last 309
A cross between two thieves ... 269	Power at Pentecost 289	Living in Rome 310
	Peter talks about Jesus 290	